STARING BACK
AT ME

TONY BIANCHI

CinnamonPress
INDEPENDENT INNOVATIVE INTERNATIONAL

Published by Cinnamon Press,
Meirion House
Tanygrisiau
Blaenau Ffestiniog
Gwynedd
LL41 3SU
www.cinnamonpress.com
The right of Tony Bianchi to be identified as the author of this work has been asserted by him in accordance with the Copyright, Designs and Patent Act, 1988. © 2018 Tony Bianchi's Estate.
ISBN 978-1-78864-010-7
British Library Cataloguing in Publication Data. A CIP record for this book can be obtained from the British Library.

Designed and typeset in Garamond by Cinnamon Press. Cover design by Adam Craig © Adam Craig.

Cinnamon Press is represented by Inpress and by the Welsh Books Council in Wales.

The publisher gratefully acknowledges the financial support of the The Welsh Books Council.

Printed in Poland.

Acknowledgements

Versions of the following stories were published in Welsh in *Cyffesion Geordie Oddi Cartref* (Gomer 2010): *Dance Ti Tha Daddy; Hunting the Octopus; Our Grandpa Who Art in Heaven; Counting to Ten; Eric 'n' Ernie; A Visit from the Police; The Bench; Learning Scriabi; Watching; Talking With the Dead*. The translations were amongst work done with the help of a bursary from Literature Wales. The author thanks that body for its support.

A Welsh version of *Skippy* won the 2013 *Taliesin*/ BBC Radio Cymru Short Story Competition and appeared in *Taliesin* magazine. *Taliesin* also published the Welsh version of *Speaking in Tongues*. *Black Spot* is based on a story included in *Fy Nghariad Cyntaf* (Gwasg y Bwthyn).

Eric 'n' Ernie was first published in English in *New Welsh Review*. *A Lost Leader* first appeared in *Planet* and *Departure* in *Lonely Crowd* (online edition).

Contents

'There isn't a great deal of difference between fact and fiction ... It's just how you choose to tell a story.'

James Frey

from Tadcu
to Hannah, Lili, Mari, Beca,
Logan, Soffia, Cai & Tomi

Staring Back at Me

Dance Ti Tha Daddy

I've just turned eight. I'm playing with Maureen over on the waste ground between our house and the old pit-heap. Maureen's brought a jam-jar to catch butterflies but I told her she'd need to put holes in the lid first, or else they'd die. That's what my brother said, you've got to put holes in the lid so that the butterflies can breathe.

'Will you put some holes in the lid for me, please, Anthony?'

But I haven't got anything to make holes with. And that's why Maureen's started to catch caterpillars and woodlice. If my brother was home I'd go and ask him, David, do we need holes for caterpillars and woodlice as well? But he's not, he's away with the Scouts. Anyway, Maureen's got three in her jam-jar already, because creepy crawlies can't get away, not like butterflies, so it's dead easy. 'That's dead easy,' I say. I tell her to put leaves in as well so they've got something to eat. Maureen's seven years old, the same as me, but she hasn't got a brother to teach her things.

Maureen pulls up some dandelion leaves and drops them into the jam-jar. She holds the jar up to the light and gives it a shake. 'They're not eating, Anthony.' She gives it another shake. 'I can't see them.' And another. 'I think they're dead. Are they dead, Anthony?'

I take the jam-jar from her. I can't see them either, but I know they're there, hiding under the leaves. I turn the jam-jar upside down. 'See?' The insects are lying on top of the leaves now, rolled into tight little balls. 'That's what they do,' I tell her. 'Just playing dead.' And I give her back the jam-jar.

'Will you put holes in?'

'Alright.'

Maureen unscrews the lid and empties the caterpillars, the woodlice and the leaves on the ground. I hunt around for something to make holes. I think perhaps a stone will do, if I can find one sharp enough. There might even be an old nail that somebody's dropped. But Judith Cunningham's here now and she's asking Maureen, 'Do you want a sweetie?' She holds out her two hands, a white paper bag in each. 'Black Bullets or Jelly Babies.'

Another girl walks over. I've not seen her before. She's got a round face and a yellow ribbon in her hair. Maureen looks at the two bags of sweets.

'You can have one of each if you want.'

Then Paul Cunningham, Judith's big brother, turns up, with his hands in his pockets, and Stephen Moat behind him. Stephen Moat lives next door to me and he's got a metal brace on his leg. 'So he doesn't grow up with a crooked leg,' Mam says. Paul and Stephen are twelve but they don't go to the same school as my brother because only Catholics are allowed into St Aiden's. Stephen's got a stick and he's hacking away at the long grass and the brambles and the nettles, sending bits of flowers and leaves up into the air. He's good at that, even though he's got a metal brace on his leg.

'Aren't you gonna offer him one?'

I don't think Paul remembers my name, so he points. He's taken the two bags of sweets from his sister now. 'Which one do you want?' he says. If they were sweets I'd got myself from the sweetshop, with my own pocket money, I'd go for the Jelly Babies. Jelly Babies are my favourites, especially the black ones. But I don't like eating other people's Jelly Babies. You can taste their fingers on them. That's why I say, 'Black Bullets, please.' Every Black Bullet's got its own little packet and you know that nobody else has touched them.

Paul Cunningham says, 'Close your eyes, then.' And I don't understand. I ask him, 'Why've I got to close me eyes?' So he says, 'Cos you're not having any sweets unless you close your eyes. Is he, Judith?' But Judith's gone off with Maureen and the new girl to chase butterflies and she doesn't hear. So Paul Cunningham turns to Stephen Moat and says, 'He doesn't get any sweets if he doesn't close his eyes, does he, Steve?' Stephen Moat says, 'You don't get anything if you don't close your eyes.' And Paul Cunningham says, 'Show him, Steve. Show him how you do it.'

Stephen closes his eyes. Paul says, 'You'd best get down on your knees as well. So we can do it properly.' Stephen kneels down and I'm surprised at that, that he can bend his gammy leg. Paul says, 'Open your mouth.' So he opens his mouth, and Paul puts a jelly baby on his tongue. Stephen's wobbling a bit now, with keeping his gammy leg bent for such a long time. And I think, he's got to open his eyes now, or else he'll fall over. But he doesn't. He stays kneeling, wobbling.

'Little prayer now, alright? Our Father ...'

Stephen tries to make the sign of the cross, but he doesn't know how and anyway I can't understand why he's trying to, because he's only eating a sweet.

'That's how you do it, Anthony, isn't it?'

And Paul Cunningham knows my name after all. So I nod. Even though I don't understand, I nod my head all the same.

'Can you do that?'

'Yes.'

'Go on, then. Down on your knees.'

I'd like to kneel down in the same place Stephen Moat kneeled down. There's more grass there, and it's flat. But he's not budged and I can't go and ask him to because he's twelve years old and he's got a metal brace on his leg. So I've got to kneel down where I am, where the ground's all stoney and bumpy.

'Black Bullet?'

'Please.'

I close my eyes and try to move my knees at the same time, because the stones are hurting and I know that I'm wobbling, just like Stephen Moat earlier on.

'Eyes shut?'

'Yes.'

'Promise?'

'Promise.'

I hear Paul Cunningham take the wrapping paper off the sweet. I open my mouth and stick out my tongue. I kneel there, trying not to wobble too much, expecting to feel the smooth hardness of the black bullet, the taste of mint as I roll it in my mouth, as I suck it.

'You peeping?'

'No.'

'Promise?'

'Promise.'

And I don't mean to peep. If Stephen Moat can do it without peeping, even though he's got a metal brace on his leg, then I'm sure I can, too, because there's nothing the matter with my legs. But I can't help it. It's not a Black Bullet in my mouth, or even a Jelly Baby, and I don't know what it is, but it's not hard or smooth or sweet. And when I open my eyes, Paul Cunningham's standing there, right in my face. His trouser buttons are open, I can see the white of his underpants, his hands are spread either side, just as if he's going for a wee. But even then, even after I've seen that he's got his flies open, that his hands are either side, I still can't work out what it is in my mouth, because I don't know what a willy in the mouth feels like, tastes like. And anyway, I'd heard him taking the wrapper off the sweet and there's a little bit of me that's still asking, *Where did the sweet go, then? What happened to the minty taste? The smooth Black Bullet?* Maureen's shouting from somewhere over in the bushes, 'Why are you peeing in his mouth, Paul?' Stephen Moat's laughing. And Paul Cunningham says, 'Well, that's it, then, you're not getting any sweets now, cos you peeped.'

And anyway, he's already put the sweet in his own mouth. I can see him now, turning it round with his tongue.

I open the kitchen door and tell Mam that Paul Cunningham's done something really yucky, but maybe I say his name before I've opened the door properly because she turns around and says, 'What did you say, Anthony? What's yucky?'

'Paul Cunningham took his ... He got his ...'

But Mam goes into the passage to talk to Dad and the words get lost. I sit at the table, wondering whether they've heard already, and that's why they've gone into the passage, to talk about it. Maybe Maureen told her mam, and Maureen's mam told my mam. I try to hear what they're saying, if I can pick out Paul Cunningham's name. But Dad's not talking about Paul Cunningham, he's talking about Mr Costa and saying he needs to get the fish. I can't hear Mam's voice, not properly, not from the passage. When she comes back into the kitchen she's already got her coat on and Dad's standing behind her, taking off his blue collar. He's finished his shift now and it's only when he's going to work that Dad wears his blue collar and the jacket with the shiny buttons.

Mam says, 'I've got to go and help your grandma. She's not well.' I ask her, 'What kind of not well?' Because I want to keep her in the kitchen. 'I've got to make your grandpa's dinner.' That's all she says. And it doesn't matter now what was yucky or who did it because she goes through the door then and doesn't look back and I don't know how to tell Dad but it won't be good enough just to say that Paul Cunningham's done something yucky, he'll want to know what and how. And am I sure? Am I really sure? I could tell him that Paul Cunningham had weed in my mouth. That's what Maureen said. But it's a big thing to say. And I've never said such a big thing before, not to Dad. Anyway, I don't know if he did wee in my mouth. When I wiped my lips afterwards I couldn't smell any wee on my fingers. When I spat it was just spit that came out.

'Come on, then. We'll go and fetch the fish.'

Dad's talking now. He's got his big blue mac on, which looks black to me, but Mam says that it's just a very very dark blue.

'Are we going to Mr Costa's?'

'Uh-huh.'

But first I've got to put a comb through my hair and clean my shoes because Dad doesn't want to go out with somebody that looks like a scarecrow.

'I know the way.'

This is the game I play when me and my Dad go and fetch the fish. 'Left here.' Then 'Straight ahead.' Then 'Cross the road by the bus stop.' I lead the way. And sometimes I go a different way, because there's lots of roads you can follow and still get to the same place. These are the same roads I take to go to school in the morning, so I know I won't get lost. And we've only got to walk straight ahead now, after we pass the school, and follow the bank down to the river, and there it is, where Mr Costa keeps his fish.

Fetching fish with Dad isn't the same as shopping with Mam. For one thing, we don't have to go to a shop. And for another, Dad doesn't pay for the fish, even when he's not in his uniform. Mr Costa knows he's got a uniform and that's enough. He wraps the fish up in paper and gives them to Dad and Dad never gives him anything back. I don't go every time, mind. But that's what happens the other times as well, I'm pretty sure. The days I'm at home and Dad comes in from work, puts his helmet on the table. Comes through the back door with the paper packet in his hand and says 'mackerel this time,' or 'herring', or 'sole', and Mam says, 'That's nice'. Nice fish. And nice to have it for nothing.

We pass the green wooden door with the Fish Merchants sign above it. We walk on a bit and turn the corner. And if we crossed the road here we'd be right by the river. You could fall in there just by walking over the edge, there's nothing to stop you. So we carry on a bit more and go in through the big sliding door that's always left open, so that the men can bring in their boxes. The men wear big aprons. Everywhere stinks of fish. And all you can hear is the banging. I don't like that sound because I know what they're doing, the men in the big aprons. I know each one's got a big sharp knife and they're chopping off the fishes' heads. Grandpa said that if I came back at dinner time, when everybody'd finished work, I'd find men's fingers all over the floor. But I've never seen anybody with bandages on their hands, so I think he was joking. We did see a shark's head once, though, me and my brother. It was over on the fish quay. Just the head, his nose stuck up in the air, his eye staring at us. I didn't like that either. But my brother said it was alright. There was a little man that worked under the quay all day and all night, holding on to the shark's tail so that it couldn't jump out and bite your legs off.

Me and Dad walk to the back, where Mr Costa's got his own little glass room. I can see through the window that Mr Costa's not there. Mr Costa's old and he's only got a little tuft off white hair on the top of his head. It's a young man that's sitting in his chair now, smoking a cigarette, talking to one of the men in big aprons. And when Dad opens the door he says, 'Wait here, Anthony,' and I'm not allowed to go in. I can hear their voices then, but I can't make out the words. The two men look at my dad. Then they look over at me, through the window, because Dad's made a sign with his thumb, has glanced over his shoulder, to show them that I'm here. The three of them laugh, and maybe I look away for a moment, to where the boxes are being loaded, I'm not sure, but when I look back they're not laughing any more and the man in the chair is shaking his head. He's saying 'No'. I can see the shape of his mouth. And shaking his head. I don't like that voice. Nobody's supposed to say 'No' to my dad.

That's when he comes out and his hands are empty. I ask him, 'Where's the fish, Dad?' But he doesn't hear. I ask him, 'Where's Mr Costa?' But all he says is, 'Come on.' Dad's leading the way now and only Dad knows where we're going. We walk over to the fish quay. I've got to run to keep up with him. And when we get there, Dad goes into Marston's Fishmonger. I can read the sign above the door. I can read lots of the things on the blackboard outside as well, that there are crabs for sale at 9d each, and other things, too, but the writing gets raggly then. And although I've got to stand outside, the door's open and I can hear my Dad asking for three lemon sole, please. She says 'one and sixpence, please.' Dad gives her the money and she wraps the fish in paper, just like Mr Costa does, to make sure the smell doesn't get on your clothes. When Dad comes out I want to ask him why he's bought the fish instead of getting them from Mr Costa. But he's looking the other way, lighting a cigarette.

We climb back up the bank from the river and Dad says, 'Here you are,' and gives me the fish to carry. And I don't like carrying fish. The paper's dry and clean on the outside but I know that the fish underneath are all soft and wet and they haven't got any heads. If I press the packet between my fingers I can feel them. And they feel yucky.

'Don't tell your Mam, mind,' Dad says. And I ask him, 'Are they the same fish, Dad? Are they the same fish we'd have got from Mr Costa?' But he doesn't answer. All he says is, 'Don't you go telling your Mam. You hear?' I don't get to play the leading-the-way game, because Dad knows the way he wants to go. 'Not a word, remember. Not a word.'

So I don't say anything about the fish. I don't tell Mam about Paul Cunningham either. I forget about Paul Cunningham. I can only think of the fish. That I mustn't mention the fish. Or Mr Costa. Or Marston's Fishmongers. And there is so much that I must remember not to remember.

Skippy

I went over to Uncle Bob's last Saturday to see him walking on his wooden leg. I took Lauren along as well in case he tried to kill me with one hand again, to show what it was like during the war. Lauren's dad's a security guard. He's big, too, and he's still got both his legs.

We looked out to make sure Gary Simmons and Paul Cunningham weren't about, then we walked over the waste ground, which was a lot quicker than going round by the streets. And when we got to the house I went straight to the back door and shouted out, 'It's me, Uncle Bob!' And rattled the sneck. Uncle Bob spent all day in his kitchen, Dad said, so there was no point going to the front and ringing the bell. 'Taken root there,' he said. I thought that was fair enough, too, what with him having a wooden leg. But I had to rattle the sneck a bit more, and knock on the door and shout out again, 'It's me here, Uncle Bob. Anthony. Come to see you.' Thinking maybe he'd gone a bit deaf since last time. He shouted back then, 'Well come on in, what you waiting for?' Except it was more a wheeze than a shout, with a bit of a cough in the middle. I opened the door and there he was, sat by the fire, reading his newspaper. I said, 'This is Lauren. Lauren's dad's a security guard.'

Uncle Bob looked at me and then at Lauren. 'My dad's Field Marshal Montgomery of Alamein. Your feet clean?' I leaned against the wall and showed him the soles of my shoes. Then Lauren did the same. It was dry out, sunny too, so there was no mud on them, even though we'd come over the waste ground. But we wiped them on the mat all the same, then walked into the warm and Uncle Bob said, 'I've got no pop, mind.'

So we stood there for a minute. Then I said, 'Shall I get some pop?'

'Get some pop?'

'From the shop,' I said, a little louder this time. 'Shall I buy some pop from the shop?'

Which made him laugh. I hadn't seen Uncle Bob laugh before. 'Pop from the shop?' he chuckled. Like little stones in a wooden box. Then coughed a bit. And thought a bit. And looked a bit, first at me, then at Lauren. And he said, 'What's one and threepence and two and sevenpence ha'penny?'

I looked up at the ceiling and said, 'Three and tenpence ha'penny.'

He was quiet then, so I thought I'd made a mistake. But now I think he was just working it out himself. And maybe he was a bit flummoxed, thinking young lads didn't do mental arithmetic any more. So then he said, 'How much change from ten bob if you buy two stotties at sixpence ha'penny each and a piece of cheese for three and fourpence?'

I was a bit longer with that one, but I got it right. Then he looked at me. 'Can you carry nails?'

'Yes,' I said.

He looked at Lauren. 'Can you carry stotties?' She nodded. 'And apples?' She nodded again.

So Uncle Bob wrote out a list and handed it over, with two fresh pound notes and a big scratchy bag that almost touched the floor. 'Don't be long,' he said.

I didn't get to see Uncle Bob walking on his wooden leg that day because me and Lauren had to go to the bakers and the greengrocers and the ironmongers, too, and that was right down at the bottom of Verne Road, and the man there wanted to know what a young lad like me was doing buying nails. I said 'Uncle Bob sent us' and held up the list. 'Clout copper,' I said, to show that me and Uncle Bob spoke the same language. 'He's building a fence.' By the time we got back and Uncle Bob had checked his change and his nails and his apples and his stotties we had to go home for our dinner, and we didn't even get to drink any of the pop we'd bought.

'Next time,' Uncle Bob said, and gave us sixpence each and an apple. 'Clout copper. Very good.'

Half term came and we set off for Uncle Bob's straight after breakfast to make sure we finished the shopping by dinnertime. He had us going over to Healy's garden shop by then, to get seeds for the spring, and down to the pet shop to buy food for his fish, and taking five pound notes as well and a bag for each hand. But that was alright because it meant Gary Simmons and Paul Cunningham weren't about yet, asking what I was doing out playing with a lass, saying I was just a big lass myself, and using rude words. So it was all for the best.

Then Uncle Bob said, 'I've got a new job for you,' and poured out two glasses of pop. He coughed a bit and poured a bottle of Stout for himself. 'For the cough,' he said. We all sat for a minute until the froth settled. I looked at his legs, tried to work out which was the wooden one, wondered why he wore a shoe on his wooden foot, and a sock as well. I think he caught me looking, so he said, 'See that pit-heap?' We both had to look through the window then. 'You been up that pit-heap?'

I said yes, I'd been up it lots of times, it was just opposite our house. 'It's flat on top,' I said, to prove it, because it didn't look flat, not from a distance, not through Uncle Bob's window, it looked round. You had to climb it to know about the flat top.

'Flat?' said Uncle Bob, and raised an eyebrow. 'What kind of flat?'

'Stones,' I said. 'The grass stops and there's lots of stones.'

'Black stones,' Lauren said.

'And red stones,' I said.

'Red stones?' said Uncle Bob, sounding surprised.

'And grey,' I said.' Black, red and grey.'

'And the red stones,' said Uncle Bob. 'Are they still hot?'

I looked at Lauren. She shook her head. 'Don't think so,' I said.

Uncle Bob looked through the window. 'Mm,' he said. 'No smoke, anyway.' Then he bent forward and took a sip from his glass. It left a rim of froth on his lip. 'So what do you see, then? Eh? What do you see when you stand on top of that pit-heap and look around you?'

I had to think about that. I looked inside my head, hoping there'd still be a picture there. And that wasn't easy. Me and Lauren didn't climb up for the view, we climbed up to see who could get to the top first.

'Our house,' I said. 'I can see our house from the top.'

'Good,' said Uncle Bob. 'Anything else?'

Lauren said, 'Mr Bibby. I can see Mr Bibby taking his dog for a walk on the waste ground.'

Uncle Bob said, 'That's good, that's very good,' and nodded his head, and waited for more, so that I had to think of something quick, before Lauren jumped in again. 'Mrs Fenby Number Four,' I said. 'I can see Mrs Fenby's garden. Her tomatoes.'

'Her tomatoes?'

'In her greenhouse. She grows tomatoes in her greenhouse. Gives them to Mam sometimes. To put in salads. To make chutney.'

Uncle Bob said, 'Chutney, good. I like a nice bit of chutney.' And coughed into his hanky. He drank the rest of his Stout and coughed again. Then he pulled two coins out of his trouser pocket and put them on the table. 'Now then,' he said. 'You go up to the top of the pit-heap after your breakfast tomorrow and come back and tell me what you can see and you'll get half a crown each. That's five bob between you. Half a dollar. Understand?'

We both nodded. We could see the half crowns on the table, so he could call them what he liked. Uncle Bob sat back for a second, then lent forward again and looked me in the eye. 'Both of you, mind. It's got to be both of you. One to look out over the waste ground. One to look out over the houses. Can you do that?'

I nodded again. Lauren nodded again. Uncle Bob sat back and gazed through the window.

'You can change places if you want, there's nothing wrong with that. Swap round. Ten minutes one way, ten minutes the other. Have a change of scenery. Yes. Might be better like that. Ten minutes one way, ten minutes the other. So you don't miss anything.' He paused and blinked. 'The eye gets lazy after ten minutes.'

I said, 'What are we looking for, Uncle Bob?'

Uncle Bob said, 'The comings and goings, Anthony. The comings and the goings.' Then he looked at Lauren. 'Your dad a security guard?'

'At Formica.' said Lauren.

'Formica? That's good,' said Uncle Bob. 'That's very good.'

The next morning, when we crossed the waste ground, I told Lauren I couldn't race today because I had to carry Mam's shopping bag with the the Five Star Wirebound Notebook in it and the pens. Lauren said, 'I'll carry them,' but I said, 'No,' because this was a job for Uncle Bob, and Uncle Bob was my uncle, not hers.

When we reached the top I pointed to the far side. 'You stand over there,' I said. 'I'll stay here.'

She looked to where I was pointing. 'There's only one book,' she said.

'Shout out,' I said. 'Shout out if you see anything and I'll write it down.'

She huffed a bit but walked over to the other side anyway because she didn't have any choice.

I took the notebook and the pens out of the shopping bag, put the bag on the ground and sat on it. Then I started looking at things. Down below I saw the path that me and Lauren had followed over the waste ground. Over in the distance was the school, with its high chimneys, its yellow and red bricks. Then, this side of the school, there were the football pitches, four of them. But there weren't any games today, with it being potato week. And I was cross with myself for not bringing gloves. There was a cold wind up here, on top of the pit-heap, even though it was sunny. The pen wouldn't work, either, and I had to scribble hard on the back of the notebook to get the ink running.

I wrote on the first page:

Sunday, 27 October

I looked at my watch, waited a few seconds until the hand reached the top, then wrote the time.

11.55 am

'It's cold.' I heard Lauren's voice from the other side. 'It's too cold to stand here.' She was hugging herself, jumping up and down, making a big fuss.

I looked down at my own house, a little off to the right: the front door, the roof, a bit of back garden.

'I said it's too cold out here.' Lauren was standing right behind me.

'You can't do that,' I said.

'Can't do what?' she said.

'You can't come over here. Not yet, not until ten minutes ...'

'But it's too cold,' she said. And blew on her hands. Stamped her feet.

'You got gloves?'

She shook her head. Then she said, 'That your mam down there?'

I didn't like that. Lauren was looking at the things I was supposed to be looking at. This side of the pit-heap was my business and she had no right to poke her nose in. She was right, though. I could see Mam, in the back garden, pegging clothes on the line. But then she disappeared, because the pit-heap wasn't high enough to see the whole garden.

'You going to write that down?'

'What?'

'Your mam, hanging the clothes out. You going to write that down in your book?'

'Course not.'

'Why not?'

'It's me Mam.'

She reached out her hand then and said, 'Let me have a go.'

I said 'No' and showed her where I'd started writing. 'Look,' I said. 'I've already started.'

But she said, 'No, you haven't, you've only written the date and the time.'

So I had to give Lauren the notebook and walk over to the other side then because I looked at my watch and ten minutes had passed and I didn't want to go back to Uncle Bob's and have to tell him we hadn't done things properly.

From the other side of the pit-heap I couldn't see my house any more, but I could see the houses opposite, or at least the backs. The sun broke through again and bounced off the glass of Mrs Fenby's greenhouse. And it was like the sun on the glass was another sun, trying to break in to get at the tomatoes. Except I think the tomatoes were probably all finished by now, with it being potato week. I needed to give my eyes a bit of a rest so I looked over at the football pitches. I wrote:

Man crossing school field with dog on lead.

Then I crossed out *dog* and wrote *labridoor*. I looked at my watch and wrote:

12.08 pm

I'd have preferred to wait until ten minutes past, to get a nice round number, but I reckoned it was best to have it right, where the comings and goings were concerned. And even though it was only a man and his dog, it was definitely a coming and going, different to Mam pegging clothes on the line.

A few minutes went by and we swapped round again. Then Lauren said it was dinner time and she had to go home. But first she came over to see what I'd written in my notebook.

'Was it Mr Bibby?'

I looked over at the fields again, but the man had gone, and his dog, too. 'I don't know,' I said. 'He was wearing a coat. A big black coat. The dog did its business in the middle of the field.'

'Its business?'

'Its dirt. It did its dirt right in the middle of the field, on the grass.'

'Where?' she said.

I looked again and had to put a hand over my eyes because of the sun, but it was too far to see anything. I said, 'Right by the goalposts.'

She said, 'That's not how you spell labrador.' She picked up a pen, put a line through what I'd written and wrote it out again, in big capitals. 'See?' she said. 'LAB—RA—DOR.' But it was all a mess now. And how could I show a mess like that to Uncle Bob?

The following Saturday Mam took the bus to town to buy shoes. She left sandwiches for dinner. It was fine so I decided to go up the pit-heap and try out the binoculars I'd had from Uncle Bob. 'So you'll have four eyes to work with,' he said. 'Brass ones, too. From the war.' But when I got them home and tried them out I found that one of the lenses had a crack in it, so it was really only three eyes . I thought, that'll be the war, more than likely. A bullet. Shrapnel. That sort of thing.

I got Dad's old haversack from the cupboard under the stairs. The binoculars were heavy so they went in first. Then I put the sandwiches into a paper bag, and a banana as well. The bag went into the sack then, and a small bottle of Tizer and a Cadbury's Skippy.

Dad was out in the garden, putting canes in the soil. 'I'm off now, Dad,' I said, through the back door. He took two shillings out of his pocket and said to get myself an ice-cream, if the van came by, or if he was out. 'Out?' I said. If he had to nip over to the garage, he said, looking at his watch. To get parts for the car. Might be some time. Saturday afternoon. Queues. Match on as well. 'Going by yourself?'

'Yes,' I said.

'Mind how you go, then.'

I didn't call on Lauren this time. There wasn't enough food for the both of us and I didn't want to share the Skippy, or the banana either. But when I came out of the house there she was, standing outside on the pavement, talking to Gary Simmons's sister. And when Gary Simmons's sister said, 'What's in the bag?' I had to show her, and not just the food either, but the binoculars as well, because I thought she might tell her brother I'd been trying to hide things. And Lauren came with me then. 'To have a look through the binoculars,' she said. Gary Simmons's sister said she'd wave up at us.

When we got to the top I opened the bag and offered Lauren a sandwich, because she'd only brought a couple of crackers. But she didn't like spam or chutney so I had to give her half a banana instead, and then the other half, because I was still eating the sandwiches and she'd finished her crackers. I kept the Skippy in the bag so I could have a treat later on. Then we each had a swig of the Tizer and I took out the binoculars.

'Let me see,' she said.

I took no notice. They were Uncle Bob's binoculars and she had no right. I closed my left eye and looked through the lens that wasn't broken. And I thought then, only two eyes really, not even three. One proper eye and one lens eye. I could see some lads kicking a ball about on the field. I turned the little wheel to get a better view. This worked fine when the ball was on the ground but I lost it then, when it went up into the air, just a tiny speck against all that sky. So I watched a motor bike instead. It was coming down Stephenson Avenue, right in front of Uncle Bob's house. I thought, Uncle Bob won't like that, a motor bike, with all its racket. But then I thought, no, he's in the back with his wooden leg. And his hearing not so clever now.

'Let me see,' Lauren said. By now Gary Simmons's sister was waving at us from below so this time I had to give her the binoculars. Then, after a bit, I heard the ice-cream van, so I took them back again, because there was no telling whether it would stop at the bottom of our street or else carry on all the way over to the kids' playground. I looked for a good while but didn't see anything, just heard the dingle-dongle dingle-dongle, quiet to begin with, then louder, then quieter again, which meant the van had already passed by. I put my hand in my pocket and felt the shilling Dad had given me and thought, 'Not to worry. I'll spend it on something else.' I opened the bag and took out the Skippy.

That's when I see Dad come out of the house and hear the door slam shut. I stand up and wave, but Dad is looking the other way. I think about shouting, but I've already noticed

Gary Simmons crossing the waste ground and I don't want him to hear. Dad's opening the front gate now, and I know what he's going to do next, he's going to walk over to the car and take it to the garage. That's what he said earlier. Had to go to the garage and get some parts.

But no, he doesn't go anywhere near the car. He crosses the road and I can't see him now because the houses are in the way. I stand on tiptoe. I walk over to the left, as far as I can go, and still nothing. Lauren shouts, 'Did you see something?' I shake my head. She shouts again. 'Yes, you did. You saw something.' I say, 'No, I didn't. I didn't see anything.'

I'm cross that I've got to share the Skippy, too. And by now it's started to go soft, with the sun's heat, with holding it in my hand. And that makes me even more cross. I like biting the chocolate off, right round, sides first, then the top, then the bottom. Lick the caramel then. Leave the biscuit till last. 'Crunch in the biscuit, munch in the middle.' That's what the advert says on the television. But all I can do today is suck it and chew it just like it was an ordinary biscuit, and the chocolate and the caramel go to slush in my mouth. I've got to swallow it too quickly then and move on to the next bit, before the chocolate goes all over my fingers.

That's when I see Dad again, down below, standing in Mrs Fenby's back garden. Mrs Fenby comes out with something in her hand. Even without the binoculars I'm pretty sure it's a cup, I can tell from the way she's holding her arm, trying not to spill anything. But I look through the binoculars anyway, just to make sure. Dad's got a cup as well. He's turned round so I can see his face, his hands, everything. And if he looked up now he'd be able to see me and Lauren, too. But he doesn't. He puts his cup down, somewhere out of sight. And I don't understand why Mrs Fenby is giving Dad her own cup. At least, that's what I think she's doing, but I can only see Dad's head and shoulders now. He's backed up against the wall, and the wall is almost as tall as he is. I turn the little wheel on the binoculars. But no, she's not giving him her cup, she's putting a hand on his arm. I can see clearly now, even though I've only got one eye and one lens. She's putting her hand on his arm, on the arm of his blue shirt. And it's too cold to be out in his shirtsleeves. That's what Mam would say, if she found out. And what is that behind his collar? Is that her other hand?

'Who's down there?'

Lauren's standing beside me. I pretend I don't hear.

'Is that your Dad down there?'

I say, 'No.'

'Yes it is,' she says. 'It's your dad. What's he doing in Mrs Fenby's garden?'

I can't think of an answer. I shrug my shoulders. Lauren holds out her hand. 'Let me see,' she says.

I say, 'No.'

'Let me,' she says again.

'Tomatoes,' I say. 'He's getting tomatoes.'

'Tomatoes?'

'Mam puts them in salads.'

She looks again. 'Give me the binoculars,' she says.

'You're not allowed,' I say. 'They're Uncle Bob's.' Which is only right, because he's my Uncle Bob, so it's me who says who can have them and when.

'Give me!' she says, and tries to grab them. I pull away. She tries again. I turn my back on her, push the binoculars into my chest, and stick out my elbows. She reaches both her arms around my middle, gets hold of my hand, digs her nails into the skin. She says, 'Give me, give me ...' I'm bent over now, Lauren's holding tight, both arms around my middle, leaning down on me, so that I almost fall over. She gets hold of my fingers and bends them back. And I've got no choice now. I swing round and hit her in the face with the binoculars. Not that I mean to, but they're in my hand, that's the way my hand goes. The edge of the binoculars hits her just by her mouth. She raises a hand but I can see the blood, it's oozing over her lips, her chin.

Lauren falls onto the stones. And that would be alright if she'd fallen on her backside. If you've got to fall, that's the best way. Sore bum, but no harm done. But she doesn't, she's falls on her head and there's nothing I can do about it. Her head is on the stones. She'll start crying soon, I know it. And I hope she won't make too much noise, or Gary Simmons might hear, and even Mrs Fenby. And it's now I see the red on my hand, then on my jacket, and the jacket's worse than the hand. I can wash my hand, but I'll get wrong off Mam for letting the blood get on the jacket.

I turn round and look out over the waste ground. Gary Simmons is sitting down, having a smoke, throwing stones into the bushes. I look the other way. Mrs Fenby's still by the greenhouse, drinking her tea. But that's alright. Lauren hasn't started crying yet, so there's nothing to hear. And I'll have to say 'Sorry, Mam', for the jacket, when I get home, when she comes back from town. I'll tell her Lauren tripped over and got a nasty cut. I was trying to help her, I'll say. And Gary Simmons. I might say something about him, too. That he was throwing stones.

But where's Dad gone? He's not in the garden any more. Mrs Fenby's drinking her tea, but where's Dad? And I'm thinking now, maybe he did look up after all, just got a glimpse of me and went back into the house. So that's something else I can say. I can say, Dad saw it all, when he came back from the garage. Lauren and the cut on her head. Gary Simmons, throwing stones. Then I'll look at Dad and he'll nod. And if he doesn't nod I'll ask him, 'Did you get tomatoes from Mrs Fenby today, Dad?' Mam will look at him. She'll say, 'Tomatoes?' Knowing it's much too late for tomatoes.

I'll take the binoculars back to Uncle Bob tomorrow. I'll say thank you, but one of the lenses is broken. And it wasn't my fault, that's how they were. I'll say, it's difficult to see with just one lens and your other eye screwed up. And I'll give them back then. I'll ask him, Was it the war? Is that how the lens got broken? And perhaps I'll see him walking on his wooden leg.

Hunting the Octopus

Mr Dixon walks up and down the rows, taps a finger on each desk as he passes, turns left or right as the whim takes him.

'Eight sevens.'

'Fifty-six, sir.'

'Six twelves.'

'Seventy-two, sir.'

'Nine nines'

'...'

Steven Dobson looks out through the window, sees grey sky, a stone wall, trees.

'Nine nines.'

'...'

Looks down, at the floor, at the toes of his black shoes.

'Dobson?'

'Seventy ...'

Steven Dobson creases his brow, tightens his lips to show Mr Dixon how hard he's trying, that the answer is in there somewhere and if he's given just one more minute to rummage around for it ...

'Eighty...'

But it's too late. This is his third error. He's already been standing by his desk for a quarter of an hour, awaiting his final chance. And yet, although he knows that no-one is ever offered more than three chances, he does not hold out his hand. Not yet, he thinks. One more go.

'Ninety ...'

He looks through the window again, parting his lips this time, as though the answer is indeed about to reveal itself and all he needs is a little more time, to consider the raindrops gathering on the window-panes, to follow the caretaker as he pushes his wheelbarrow across the yard with its load of twigs and leaves. Or as though he is waiting for

Zorro to appear, sword-in-hand, and whisk him away on his black horse, take him somewhere far that doesn't smell of chalk and ink and damp coats. As though he believes, in all sincerity, that he can bide his time until Mr Dixon loses interest and turns to someone else, that maybe the bell will ring, and he will be saved.

We all know that Mr Dixon won't lose interest. We watch the cane, in the air now, tight in his fist, ready to strike. There's no sign of Zorro. The correct answer doesn't land on Dobson's head like the Holy Paraclete. Worst of all, his brain has ceased to function. It lies, inert, in the caretaker's wheelbarrow, together with the twigs and leaves.

'Ninety-nine, sir?'

The miracle doesn't happen. Even in a Catholic school, miracles are not allowed to interfere with good order and discipline.

'Tell him, Bianchi.'

'Nine nines eighty-one, sir.'

The cane strikes Dobson's hand. He is lucky. Sometimes Mr Dixon aims for the finger-tips. Today, Dobson's palm takes the full blow. This cannot be ascribed to any lapse or imprecision in Mr Dixon's aim. Nor is it the result of Dobson moving his hand at the last minute, as some pupils do, in their folly, only to be compelled then to suffer a second and more severe strike. No, Mr Dixon aims for the palm of Steven Dobson's hand because it's Friday. He's in a good mood. He feels disposed to show clemency.

Dobson presses his hand under his armpit. He's relieved the worst is over. Only the pain remains.

'Nine nines?'

'Eighty-one, sir.'

'Say it.'

'Nine nines eighty-one, sir.'

Standard IV does mental arithmetic every Friday morning. Every Monday morning, too. Mr Dixon tells them it is the best practice for the 11 Plus, that they'll thank him in years to come. Also, he says, it will keep their minds alert over the weekend. And when Monday comes, it will help wake them up again. Otherwise, he says, the minds of all the little boys will return to their primordial state. Their original condition, he says, when all the world's children lived amongst the beasts of the swamp and the slime.

'Which beasts, Milne?'

'The beasts of the swamp and the slime, sir.'

'Name one of the beasts of the swamp and the slime, Taylor.'

'I don't know, sir.'

'Don't know? What, not one? Shame on you, Taylor. And what about you, Askew? Can you name one of the beasts of the swamp and the slime?'

'No, sir.'

'On your feet, Askew. Answer on your feet.'

'No, sir.'

'No? Well, that's a surprise. Haven't you heard of the Giant Sloth?'

'No, sir.'

'Yes, a big surprise. What with the two of you being so closely related.'

We laugh. We chew over the word 'sloth' in our minds. 'Slimy sloth,' we think. We are glad to have a new name to call the fat boy who smells of potatoes.

I've no doubt that mental arithmetic spoils the weekend for some: that Friday's sums will buzz stubbornly in their heads as they get ready for Saturday football; that the prospect of Monday's calculations will cast a shadow over their Sunday evening television. But I am indifferent to their concerns. I'm good at doing sums in my head, and learning tables, and things of that sort, and I've never had to stand up in class. Not once. Let alone put out my hand.

And it pains me to say this, but I actually derive some strange satisfaction from seeing Dobson submit to his punishment. Not only Dobson, of course, but also Milne, when his turn comes. And Lake and Kelly and McKenna and Bolger and the others. Because it's same boys who are called to their feet every week, as though preordained. I feel a little frisson as the cane strikes the hand, taste the relief that I am once more exempt. I hold my hands together under the desk, savour their lack of pain, their freedom from guilt.

In the afternoon we learn opposites.
    'Home.'
    'Abroad.'
    'Front.'
    'Back.'
    'Guilty.'
    'Innocent.'
    'Wax.'
    'Wane.'
We recite them, then write them down in two columns in our exercise books, just like they are in *First Aid to English*.

Our school has four classrooms and a hall in the middle. The internal walls—really more partitions than walls—are of wood, all in a dark brown varnish. Both the partitions and the doors have windows in their upper panels. While we copy down the words, Mr Dixon walks over to the door and looks through one of those windows. Peter Lister says he's looking at Mrs Pantrini when he does that. Mrs Pantrini teaches Standard II. And that's why he's smiling now, as he stands there, by the door, because Mrs Pantrini's winking back at him. Only Peter Lister knows this. He saw them one morning, he says, when he was late getting to school. Came into the hall and there they were, Mr Dixon and Mrs Pantrini, winking at each other, smiling, from one room to the other.

'What are your balls for?'

Peter Lister knows things.

'What?'

Mr Dixon has left the room, but we still whisper.

'What are your balls for?'

Peter Lister turns to the desk behind him, where Paul White and Kevin Spencer are flicking rolled up pieces of paper at each other. 'Hey! Bianchi doesn't know what his balls are for!'

White and Spencer try to suppress their laughter.

'Everybody knows what their balls are for,' says White.

'You'd die without your balls, man,' says Spencer.

They whisper, too, because there's no telling when Mr Dixon will return, and anyway he's left the door open. They whisper behind their hands, keep an eye on the door, on the windows in the partition, knowing that Mr Dixon sometimes has a sly peep, tries to catch us out.

Mrs Pantrini rings the Angelus bell. It's a hand bell, the same bell that calls us in from the yard in the morning. But Mrs Armstrong rings the morning bell. The Angelus bell is Mrs Pantrini's responsibility.

'The Angel of the Lord declared unto Mary ...'

We stand up, join our hands together and look up at the statue of Our Lady that stands on a little shelf in the corner of the room. She reaches out her hands, tilts her head, welcomes our attentions.

'And she conceived of the Holy Ghost.'

And since Mr Dixon, for these few seconds, has his back turned to us, Kelly and Goldstone—as well as some others, no doubt, but these are the ones I see from my desk —start making faces at each other. They do so behind their hands, just in case. They make faces and say their prayers at the same time. Askew picks his nose and flicks the snot at Tracey; smears a bogey on his jumper.

'Pour forth we beseech Thee, O Lord, Thy grace into our hearts, that we, to whom the Incarnation of Christ Thy Son was made known by the message of an angel, may by His Passion and Cross be brought to the glory of His Resurrection. Through the same Christ Our Lord.'

'Amen.'

Harry Lake laughs. It's easy to make Harry Lake laugh; and once he's started, he can't stop. Short and plump, he has a cherubic face. Everyone calls him Charlie Drake, because the names rhyme, and because their bodies rhyme, too, and their bubbling chuckles. When he laughs like that on the yard we shout out 'Hello, my darlings!' Not here, though, not in the classroom.

Mr Dixon recognises that laugh. Without turning, without disturbing a syllable of his homage to God's mother, he pins the voice down. So when the prayer comes to an end and we resume our seats, he makes straight for the third desk in the second row and asks Harry Lake whether he knows the meaning of the words, 'His Passion and Cross'. He asks him whether he considers it appropriate behaviour, to laugh whilst his Saviour writhes in agony on the Cross. Yes, writhes and groans still, as though those brutal Roman soldiers had never ceased their vicious flagellation.

'His Passion and Cross, Lake. His Passion and Cross.'

Although Harry Lake has stopped laughing he still resembles a cherub. An anxious cherub. And I don't think Mr Dixon likes that: the sweetly innocent cast of Harry Lake's face which, despite his best efforts, seems to abjure the penitential submission that the situation properly demands.

'What were you laughing at, Lake?

Harry Lake does not answer. Harry Lake cannot answer. Mr Dixon has filled his head with God and big words so how can he possibly start talking about snot and pulling faces? Not that he wishes to be disobedient. Indeed, he is not at all stubborn by nature. He has no inclination to rebel. He is prone to laughter, nothing more. And at this moment he desires only to conform. But he cannot speak. His head is full of God's big words. His mouth is dry, his tongue has turned to stone.

Mr Dixon returns to the front of the class. He tells us to get to our feet, to stand in the aisles between our desks and stretch out our arms. 'Without touching your neighbour,' he adds. We obey. We stretch out our arms. And it requires considerable foot-shuffling to do so satisfactorily. There are thirty-eight of us in the class, the desks are big, the aisles narrow, and there's very little room left to accommodate such a manoeuvre.

Once we have stretched out our arms, Mr Dixon says, 'There you are, that's what it was like for Jesus on his Cross. No, no, Askew, you can't drop them yet. Jesus Christ didn't get to drop his arms for three whole days. Think of it, Askew. Three whole days and nights. No, Kelly. You can't raise them either. Don't you remember the nails? Don't you recall having those big iron nails hammered through your hands, pinning you tight to the wood? Six inch nails. Just think of it.'

Mr Dixon walks slowly down each aisle, uses the point of his cane to raise a hand here, lower a hand there, just enough to keep our arms level. Our fingers are trembling a little by now. But no, we're not allowed to tremble either. Mr Dixon says so. How can you even tremble with those great nails holding you fast to the wood? He's said this already and he's not going to say it again.

But whatever Mr Dixon chooses to say, our fingers tremble regardless. The fingers themselves feel no pain, of course—this is concentrated in the upper arms and shoulders—but it is there, in the fingers' pathetic fluttering, that the pain is made manifest. I look sideways, left then right, and try to will them into submission. But it's no use. I'm good at doing sums but I have little aptitude at cricket and rounders and things of that sort, the things that would have given my arms the muscles they most need now, here, hanging on the Cross.

And then, a minute later, it is just as though there were someone here, standing behind me, trying to pull my arms down. I no longer have nails in my hands, I have two tight cords tied around my wrists, a big heavy brick suspended from each. And perhaps that would be fine if there were two other cords pulling in the opposite direction, if there were someone above, hanging from the ceiling, say, fishing rod in hand, neatly hooking my shirt sleeves, pulling them back up again. Something, anything, to lighten the load, because the load has become very heavy now, unbearably heavy, the fingers are fluttering like little sparrow wings.

But that, too, would be a miracle.

We all like Friday because, come three o'clock, we put our work books away and Mr Dixon sits on his desk and reads a story from *A Pattern of Islands*. This is my favourite book. And although I've heard all the stories before—I'm well in to my second year in Standard IV—this familiarity somehow only whets my appetite, heightens the thrill of escaping to a sunnier world where the children go to the beach every day and there's never any mention of school or crosses or six-inch nails.

Mr Dixon is reading 'Assignment with an Octopus' today. The meat of the *Octopus Vulgaris* is a delicacy amongst the Gilbert Islanders, says the author, and every native boy learns how to hunt it. By the time he's seventeen, catching an octopus is as easy as picking an apple from a tree. Which doesn't mean it isn't a dangerous enterprise, more dangerous than anything he has previously attempted. In pursuing an octopus, for example, he must be especially vigilant in protecting the eyes: if a sucker attaches itself to the eyeball it cannot be removed. Even amputation of the octopus's limb would be of no avail. And there you'd be, an eye the poorer, the islanders a meal the hungrier. This is what the author says. Some of us cover our eyes, feel the tug on the jelly. And this is only one of many perils.

I swim with the author to the crack in the reef where the creature has made his lair. This is the custom of the *Octopus Vulgaris*. He eats his fill of crabs and lobsters then seeks a sheltered recess to digest his meal, perhaps to steal a little nap, safe from predators. I swim, my eyes just an inch or two beneath the surface of the water, seeking out nooks and crannies, watching out for the least twitch, the merest tremble, the slightest hint of a tentacle, poking out, testing the waters. I must remember that the octopus, for all the great feast he has just enjoyed, is always game for a little supplementary delicacy. And this, you might say, is the most dangerous predator of all: his own insatiable greed.

Do I spot a tentacle? Or is it only a fish? Or the fronds of a plant? It's difficult to say. Everything is so unfamiliar here. Everything is of the water, undulating with its swell, obeying laws quite alien to us, clumsy, tripping creatures of the dry land. But yes, it is a tentacle, I can see now, the author is showing it to us, inviting us to follow. This is how you hunt an octopus in these islands, he says. See the tentacle twitch, just the tip, as it peeks out from its hiding place. Then make your kill.

And as I have heard this story before, I obey without fear or apprehension. I follow the author to the crack in the reef. Once I have secured my position—I am now shuffling in my seat, full of excitement at what is to follow—I begin to dance. Yes, I dance in the water. Shake my arms, kick my feet, wiggle my head, my fingers—to show the monster how delectably wriggly, how ecstatically tasty is the strange fish that has suddenly manifested itself before him. But I cover my eyes all the while, just peep through the fingers. I mustn't forget that. The hand over the eyes.

At first the creature fails to respond. Perhaps he even retreats a little, wary of such a bold and unconventional adversary. I must persevere. I go closer. I am now so close that I could, if I wished, give his nose a little tweak between my finger and thumb. I wriggle more vigorously, more frantically, just as though I were live bait on a hook. Eventually, after much perseverance, the octopus yields to its deepest instincts. Hunger, in the end, always triumphs over fear. The islanders know this. I know this, too. I have lived this story many times.

A tentacle wraps itself around my right arm, another around my waist. This will all be to my advantage in the long run, of course, because in seizing his new prey the octopus must loosen his grip on the coral. Nevertheless, it is not a pleasant feeling, to have his tentacles looping around me, getting tighter and tighter, their suckers pulling on my skin. I need to exercise great restraint in order not to fight back. That is what is natural, after all: to retaliate, to pull myself free, to do something—anything—to save myself. But no, I hold my nerve, I prove that I am not bound by such primitive instincts, that I am in every way superior to the beast with whom I have entered mortal combat. I hold my breath. And that is the hardest thing of all. The lungs screaming for air.

After pausing briefly to secure his hold, the octopus pulls me towards the crack. This is the crux moment, the point of no return. The horned mouth sucks the skin at my stomach. My head and shoulders have already been swallowed up by the dark recess. And that is when my friend, my fellow hunter, comes to my aid. He's right behind me. In fact, he's been there all the while, biding his time. He takes hold of my left arm and with a single, sudden tug pulls me towards him. Fearing his prey is about to escape, the octopus wraps a tentacle around my shoulders and another around my right leg so that, quite inadvertently, he relinquishes his purchase on the coral. How easy it is then to pluck him from his refuge. A little kick and all three of us—me, my friend, the greedy octopus

—are on the surface of the water. I can breathe now, I am back in my own habitat, the struggle almost over. My friend closes his fingers around the top of the creature's head and draws it towards him. For a brief second, hunter and hunted stare each other in the eye. Then, in a single movement, and channelling the strength of his whole body, my friend sinks his teeth deep into the head's rubbery flesh. It is all over. The octopus gives up the ghost. We take its body home for supper.

Child's play.

Everyone in the class thinks, that must be a really gruesome thing to do, to sink your teeth into the head of an octopus, to chew its brains. They ask Mr Dixon, What did it taste like, sir? Did blood come out? Was it red? Was it the same colour as our blood? And what would have happened if the friend hadn't turned up, or had been just a few seconds late? But we're all glad, in the end, that the animal is dead, that we've learned how to kill an octopus.

I like Friday afternoon because we get to go home half an hour early and because I've got the whole weekend in front of me, playing football tomorrow, going to the Spanish City on Sunday, spending my pocket money. And even this evening, after I've gone home, everything will be alright, because Dad's on nightshift and I'll be in bed long before he gets back.

Counting to Ten

8.00

Come for a walk on the terrace, to keep warm, to watch the boys playing on the yard below. But don't walk too fast. The Canon's on duty this morning and you mustn't draw attention to yourself. And don't walk too slowly, either, because that would have the same result. You'd catch each other up and come face-to-face. I'm not sure what would happen then, what he would do if he saw you, a stranger, an interloper, on his property, but he wouldn't be best pleased. I dare say you'd be none too impressed yourself, for the Canon is a daunting figure, especially to those unfamiliar with true godliness. The Canon has no lips. He has a beak, narrow and pointed, and a bald, grey head. His face, too, is grey, there is no pink in sight, not even at the neck, where you'd imagine a vein must pulse somewhere.

The hands as well, folded behind his back; even the ears, unmoved by the chill air: all is grey, a frugal dilution of the black cassock he always wears, winter and summer, so you wonder, what is underneath? And is that grey, too? Come to think of it, perhaps you'd be best advised to sit down on one of the wooden benches. You'll blend in better there. And remember to put your hands in your pockets, against the cold.

It's eight o'clock in the morning. The bell won't ring for another hour and ten minutes but some boys are already down there, on the yard, putting their bags and jackets on the wall, kicking a ball. These are the Denton and Benwell contingents. Scotswood, too, perhaps. I say 'perhaps' because I am imagining these things. My home is in North Shields, which is over an hour's journey away, so I'm on the bus, checking my homework, letting my mind wander. Nevertheless, I'm confident that this is the shape of things on the school yard this morning, that this is how it must be every Monday morning. The early arrivals. Only seven, you can count them in a single blink. Their football. The Canon, patrolling his terrace.

But on second thoughts, not quite all grey, either. The Canon's eyebrows are black. Only the eyebrows. As though the cassock has seeped through somehow, undiluted, distilled.

8.10

There are now twelve boys on the yard. This is better. Half an acre is much too big for seven, even if they are fourth formers and wearing long trousers. Fairer, too. Six against six. And a better calibre of play, a greater impulse to compete, to pass and mark and defend as though it were a real game and the result mattered. Look. Do you see the stocky lad, down below you on the left? Spillman is his name. Keep an eye on him. He has talent. Watch how he picks out his team-mate, over on the other side of the yard.

Just a quick glance. Pauses. Balances himself. He's seen Alan Suddick do this at St James's Park: last Saturday, perhaps, against Charlton. He's seen him thread the ball through for Barry Thomas, arms down by his side all the while, giving nothing away. He does likewise. Just one glance, a quick stab of the foot. His team mate runs through, drops a shoulder, steers the ball past two defenders.

I imagine these things, how it must be, before I arrive.

8.17

The sun, bright but without warmth, has just risen above the priests' house. It makes the frost on the gymnasium roof sparkle, rolls back the long shadow from the football fields, inch by inch. The boys blow little clouds as they run. There are now more than thirty of them on the yard: too many to count with any accuracy as they weave between each other, chasing the ball, seeking a better position. And too many, you might suppose, for a satisfactory game of football on what is, after all, a quite meagre strip of concrete. But they get by. Which is quite impressive, really. And perhaps fully to appreciate what a remarkable feat this is, you need to take up a different vantage point. I suggest, therefore, that you leave your bench on the terrace and spend a little time amongst the birds. You're lucky today. They've promised snow and the gulls have retreated inland. Do you see them circling above? Herring gulls, I think. Choose one. Borrow his eyes.

8.30

That's more like it. You can look down now and see all the boys in a single glance. Notice how the original game continues more or less as before, except that the number of participants has increased again, perhaps even doubled. By now, however—and this is really why I've given you the herring gull's eyes—you will notice that another game has begun, and that this game is being played, not from one end of the yard to the other, imitating a real football match on a real pitch, but rather from side to side. These, the side-to-side players, are from Jesmond, Benton and Heaton. It's half past eight, and they have slightly further to travel. They must make do with second best.

And even from the air, with your sharp avian eyes, it is not always easy to distinguish the boys in the first game from those in the second. They are, after all, wearing the same grey shirts and trousers, the same striped ties; they are all running, shouting, waving their arms, kicking and tackling. Persevere. Hold your gaze. As the minutes pass, you will begin to recognise those tell-tale patterns that signify order, purpose and collaboration; that there are two such orders, occupying the same space yet quite distinct.

First, you will identify the two balls. The early arrivals' ball is blue; their successors' is brown. The latter is also somewhat larger. In addition, as I have already mentioned, the two games are being played at right angles to each other. And although players in all four teams frequently cross each others' paths—this is inevitable when fifty children are gathered together in such a small space—it is quite clear that each has his specific orientation and purpose, that each game has its own ebb and flow. Yes, that's good. Ebb and flow. That's how a seagull would see things.

8.43
There are fifty boys by now, perhaps more. It's turned twenty to nine and more and more of them are teeming onto the yard. The later boys would, I've no doubt, prefer to play football on the fields just the other side of the yard. These are big, empty and inviting, and at the moment not at all muddy. That, however, is not possible. Only during designated games periods and officially sanctioned matches are they permitted to venture onto the grass. Even the grass between the pitches is forbidden territory.

You are still in the air, with the gulls, looking down on the boys. Looking down, too, on the Canon's bald skull, as he walks back and forth in his black cassock, keeping his own watch. And perhaps, between his sharp beak and his see-all-eyes he has more right than you to call himself a bird. But not the same kind of bird, of course. If you are a seagull, the Canon would be a crow.

Five games are in progress now. And although you can still encompass all in a single glance, it has become increasingly difficult to distinguish between them, to pick out their defining patterns. They are there, of course. Each boy knows to whom he's trying to pass the ball, at which goal he must aim his shots. Fishwick, for example, knows that it is the yellow ball, and the yellow ball alone, that he is allowed to touch. Notwithstanding the tumult around him, he traces the pattern only of the game in which he participates. Each knows his game, and no other. Which begs the question then whether it is possible for anyone to know more than one such game, to see all the patterns at the same time and understand their progress. For seeing and understanding are quite different matters. That is why you must be a particularly diligent and observant seagull to make sense of the frenzy below, to follow the course not only of the yellow and brown balls, but also the red and the green and the white and the slightly smaller brown, and so on. To follow them and understand the logic of their motion.

8.45

I mean, to understand, and then to remember, for of what use is understanding unless it can be recalled? So, to help you remember, I propose that you draw a picture. Please decide for yourself what kind of picture you would prefer, but be warned, a photograph will not do. A photograph is no better than an eye for understanding the logic of moving things. To save time, I shall tell you what my own choice would be. Thread. Thread would be my preference. I urge you to follow suit. The boys weave between each other on the school yard. Through picturing them in thread, you too may weave.

This is how it works. Draw a thread along the path of one of the balls—let's say the red ball—and in a short while you will have a fixed record of that game's progress, a visible representation of its transient patterns. To do this properly you will also need some pins. These will allow you to show all the twists and turns the ball takes on its way between one goal and the other, the sometimes meandering, faltering or frustrated dribbles of the forwards, the desperate clearances of the defenders, and so on. You'll have to get a board as well, of course, to stick the pins into: nothing too fancy—an old piece of plywood will do—but its dimensions will have to correspond to those of the yard itself. And that's the red game done.

Then you'll need to take another thread and do the same with the yellow ball. And another thread, and another, until all the balls have been followed, each game, each player traced and pinned down. Remember to use threads of different colours, so that you may differentiate between the games. For convenience I suggest you match the colour of a thread to that of the ball it represents, yellow for the first, brown for the second, and so on. As for the other brown ball, the smaller one, perhaps a thread of lesser denier will suffice, or a thread of lighter hue. You must use your imagination, adapt my suggestions to your circumstances and resources. And in this way, having woven the path of each and every ball, you will in quite a short while hold before you the warp and weft of the school yard's early morning in all its colourful exuberance. Indeed, once the job is done, that is probably all you will see: you will forget about the football and the footballers alike, your attention will be taken up entirely by the threads, the fine homespun that your eye has woven, like a shuttle in a loom.

after all, and today I fancy playing referee. It isn't as good as showing off my dribbling skills or scoring goals, but it's better than sitting on the terrace, watching, shivering.

'I'll be ref.' And I tell Turnbull because he is the best player in this game. He doesn't play for the school, he doesn't even play for his house, but he's miles better than the others and that's all that counts. Through telling Turnbull, I tell them all. One or two—Murphy and Anderson, in particular—seem content, judging no doubt that having a referee raises their game to a higher level. They acknowledge my role from the outset, throw themselves into the spirit of our little experiment. 'Hand ball, ref!' one of them shouts. 'Accidental, man!' shouts another. And when I raise my arm—that is, the arm that is encased in plaster, for it is this arm, to my mind, which best represents my authority—they submit graciously enough to my judgement, barring only the usual ritual demur.

As for the others, I'm not so sure. Sumner has always had a moody streak and I expected little response from him, positive or otherwise. Added to which, I don't have a whistle. And the lack of a whistle provides a ready excuse for the more recalcitrant individuals to ignore my adjudications. With foresight, I should have bought something over the weekend. It occurs to me now that a recorder might just do the trick: not the whole instrument, of course, only the bore. A single, clear, high note is what we need, after all, not a rendition of *Frère Jacques* or *Pop Goes the Weasel*. But my recorder is at home, on the little square table by my bedside. And it's too late to borrow another.

So, instead of whistling, I decide to shout. My voice has broken early and I'm confident I can bawl out 'Foul!' with as much conviction as any of my age-group, and louder than most. 'Voice like a fog-horn,' Mam says. So that is what I do. I shout 'Foul!' at the first opportunity. Sumner has tugged Turnbull's shirt: a minor and ineffective infringement, but a useful test case, nonetheless. And again,

'Foul!' But it is quite futile. My voice, loud though it may be, is but one among many. Thrown across such a sea of yelps and ululations, it sinks without trace. I try again, this time running to the scene of the crime and raising my arm in the air, just like the real referees do. 'Foul! Foul!' I cry. But the ball has already been passed to someone else, the game is following its course and I have lost the thread entirely.

8.53

This is why I have devised a more radical method of exerting control.

Anderson trips Murphy. I run towards him and shout 'Foul!', as before. This time, however, in addition to shouting, I bend down and pick up the ball. I need to be quick and nimble to do so—in fact, so swift is my swoop, I almost lose my glasses—but I have the advantage of surprise on my side. The game comes to an abrupt stop. Of course it does. No ball, no game. And perhaps, on this first occasion, my action is prompted more by impatience than strategic thinking: I am frustrated at my peers' lack of respect for the rules of the game. And yes, I readily confess, perhaps I am also peeved at my own failure, my inability to command obedience from the more wilful members of our two teams. But then, as soon is the ball is in my grasp, all becomes clear. For therein lies the secret. It is not the man that must be pursued in order to bring the game under control, but rather the ball.

9.05

And if you get up from your seat and look over slightly to the left, you'll be able to pick me out. I'm the boy—the only boy—who's standing still, while all mill around. My injured arm is in the air; the other holds the ball. Anderson can protest as much as he likes. Sumner can do his arms-on-hips pouty look, just like Ollie Burton does at St James's

Park. Keelor can shout in my ear that it's his ball, not mine, as though that made any difference, as though *that* gave him carte blanche. But they all relent in the end. They can't play without a ball, and none is so barbarous as to use physical force on a boy whose arm is encased in plaster. I stand, unmoved.

Once everyone has calmed down I put the ball back on the ground at the exact point where the foul was committed. (Anderson is guilty of hand-ball: a common enough occurrence here, amongst the unintended cannons and ricochets.) Then I measure the minimum distance to which the opposition players must retreat. You may think this somewhat pedantic for a school playground kick-about, but if one rule is ignored, then what hope is there for the others? A rule is a rule. You can't pick and choose.

I place the ball on the ground, at the appropriate spot, and take bold, deliberate steps.

One ... two ... three ...

I take bolder and bigger steps than normal, too, because the steps of an eleven-year-old boy, even one quite tall for his age, scarcely meet the requirements of the regulations.

... four ... five ... six ...

And perhaps you will judge, from your vantage point up on the terrace, that there is a something of a jump about each of these steps. So be it. If a little jump is required to achieve the full yard, who can complain? A yard is a yard, not two foot seven inches. And what is the point of measuring if the measurements are false?

... seven ... eight ... nine ...

9.10

I am much disappointed, therefore, at the count of nine, when I turn and see Turnbull kick the ball. When I see Keelor, a moment later, a mere two yards away, stretch out his left leg and block the ball with his shin. When, as a result, the ball careers over to the other side of the yard and all run off in hot pursuit, like wild dogs.

I shout. 'I haven't counted to ten!'

But no-one hears. I run after the ball and shout again. 'You've got to take the free kick again. I haven't counted to ten!'

I shout louder than ever, because I'm getting cross. I'm losing patience with their arrogance, their lack of respect, not for me but for the rules of the game. A game without rules is no game at all.

'I haven't counted to ten!'

I shout as loud as I can. So loud, and with such vehemence, that I fail to hear the morning bell, that I don't notice the ensuing silence, nor my voice, tearing that silence apart. I notice nothing until Sumner's gaze is upon me. Then Turnbull's and Keelor's and Murphy's. Then the boys at the far end of the yard: they, too, gathering their bags and blazers, turn and stare.

'I haven't counted to ten!'

Even the Canon himself, up on his terrace. He turns his beak on me. His lipless mouth. His see-all eyes.

And the first snow-flakes fall.

Our Grandpa, Who Art in Heaven

Grandpa's sitting at the organ, pulling out the stops for the first hymn. Tock ... Tock ... Tock ... But I don't think he's pulling them all out, because this is a big organ and our voices are few. Tock ... Tock... I feel the tip of his finger on my shoulder. I turn around, take the half crown and whisper, 'Thank you.'

Grandpa looks in the mirror above him, waits for the vestry door to open, the priest to appear. His hands are ready to strike the first chord. Somewhere, out of sight, I hear the purring of the pump.

Here's a picture of my grandfather, Thomas Nesbitt. He was organist at St Cuthbert's for 60 years. The picture was published in the *North Shields Evening News* to mark his retirement. Although it is clearly posed—there's no music on the stand and organists don't, as a rule, look sideways while playing their instrument—it still conveys something of the character of the man. Note the half smile, and the playful way he raises his left eyebrow: both features bear witness to his humour and lively intelligence. Note also the eyes and fingers. There is confidence here still: the certainty that this is his natural habitat.

And I've no doubt that my grandfather could have played on for another two or three years. His musical abilities were still intact and he was sprightly for his age. But it wasn't to be. The parish priest, Father Hedley, decided the time had come to give someone younger a chance, that it would be best for my grandfather if he vacated his post now, while still 'on top form', as he put it. Perhaps he feared that the young musician he had in mind might take his talents elsewhere if he didn't snap him up promptly. I can't be sure. My grandfather accepted his fate. He received a wireless in recognition of his services. His photograph appeared in the local paper.

I would see my grandfather at Sunday evening benediction. If the picture were a little wider you could make out where I used to sit, in the back row of the gallery. When I turned, I was close enough to the organ to read the writing on the stops. The *Open Diapason 16*, the *Bourdon 16*, the *Principal 8*, the *Flute 8* and so on. And if I lent over a little I could even read the words on the little brass plaque set into the dark wood.

> Built and Maintained
> by
> H. E. Prested of Durham

Close enough, too, so that, a few minutes before the service started, my grandfather could tap my shoulder and give me half a crown, without even turning round or saying a single word. Although he was indeed a man of accomplishment, he was also modest and never courted attention.

As the vestry door opens and the priest emerges, golden coped, followed by four altar-boys in their white surplices, Grandpa strikes the first chords. The church fills with their soft, comforting resonance. Here in the gallery, however, the low notes are not sounds but rather tremors in the wooden floor. The higher notes take flight, settle in the roof, far from Grandpa's fingers. And it is hard to believe that one man can hold all these things together in such perfect balance.

I alone, of the whole congregation, was allowed to sit in the gallery for benediction. I enjoyed a right of inheritance, you might say. Not only was I related to the organist, but my grandmother led the choir and my mother had been a stalwart of the soprano section since childhood. Not that I was a mere observer. Although not a formal member of the choir, I sang along as best I could. And a little ballast was always welcome. The choir was by then a much diminished shadow of its former self. The days of the big masses—the Haydn, the Gounod and the Hummel—had long gone. No-one had joined for a decade; several had died or become infirm. Soon the choir would be ousted altogether, by guitars and unfettered participation. But for the time being I filled a little gap. My voice, newly broken, was strong for a thirteen year old, and I sang with zeal.

I felt privileged, too, because I sat near the seat of power. To those down below, in the common pews, the organ was no less than the voice of God Himself, out of sight but ever-present, known only through its great trembling bass, its ethereal descants. Up here in the gallery, of course, I only had to turn to see my grandfather's shiny black shoes dancing up and down the pedals and know that it was all a trick. But magic is seductive. Which no doubt is why he derived such pleasure from playing the organ and why he would never voluntarily have relinquished his position. For who else, in our church, could perform such wonders? Not Father Hedley, for sure. Our parish priest struggled to get through the litany, and that was just two or three notes. And although my grandfather would never himself have uttered anything so blasphemous, I do wonder whether part of him chuckled sometimes at seeing God Himself locked away in His little box on the altar, while he took centre stage. It was my grandfather, not God, who was the true master of miracles in this crumbling temple of ours.

Father Hedley and his four assistants kneel before the altar. We sing the litany, Father Hedley leading in his reedy tenor, choir and congregation responding. Is there a congregation? I can't see anyone, not from this vantage point, and I don't think I can hear anyone either. I hear only our voices, Grandma's choir. But they must be there, out of sight and sound, otherwise what would be the point? Anyway, I give them no thought. I am content, here in my own little heaven, savouring the nutty Latin consonants, swaying gently to the hypnotic repetitions.

Regina martyrum
   ora pro nobis.
   Regina confessorum
   ora pro nobis.
   Regina virginum
   ora pro nobis.
   Regina sine labe originali concepta
   ora pro nobis.

My grandfather thought he was privileged, too. The facts, as I had them from Mam, bore him out. Not that this was clear at the outset. Indeed, if you consider his family history, you might have predicted a bleak future for him. His mother died when he was five. A few months later, his father succumbed to the Russian flu. One brother, Robert, was blown to pieces at Ypres, while another perished in infancy. Such an orgy of death would have broken the spirit of many. But not my grandfather. Whether he missed his family I cannot say, but he never mentioned them. In fact, I don't remember him indulging in any form of nostalgia or self-pity. He lived in the present and seemed content with his lot. He had survived. God had spared him. That was sufficient.

There was only one other person whom my grandfather considered more blessed than himself and that was his sister, Elizabeth. At twenty years of age, Elizabeth had started coughing blood and it was thought to be only a matter of time before she followed her parents and brothers to a premature grave. Then, at the eleventh hour, she visited Fatima and was blessed with a miraculous cure. She coughed blood no more and lived on until she was almost as old as Grandpa himself, an object of reverence and wonderment amongst all who knew her. And yet I'm sure my grandfather was never jealous. After returning from Portugal, Elizabeth entered a convent, by way of saying thank you to God for His mercy. She then spent the rest of her days preparing for the death which she had prayed so earnestly to be spared. This would have run counter to my grandfather's rational instincts, not to mention his love of life. Although quite orthodox in matters of theology, he would have been very ill-suited to the strictures of the cloister.

Here is a photograph of the two of them together. It must have been taken during a visit to the Sisters of Mercy convent in Worthing: some time in the early 1920s, I would guess, judging by the spats. Although the picture is a little unclear, you can discern that tell-tale half smile, the penetrating eyes, the confident bearing.

Father Hedley is standing on the top step of the altar, wrapping the humeral veil around his hands. He raises the monstrance and turns to the congregation. And if the worshippers were to take a peek now, they would see him use the monstrance to make the sign of the cross and bring the Lord's blessings upon them. They would see the flashes as the golden spikes catch the lights of the sanctuary. But no-one peeks. Even here, compressed into a thin little wafer, God is much too big, much too bright to be viewed by the sons and daughters of Cain. So they keep their heads bowed, their eyes shut. They worship the great unseen. The altar boys, too, abase themselves; all except the thurefer, and I doubt whether he sees much through the fog of incense. But

although we see nothing, we hear his thurible's clack-clack, clack-clack, we smell the incense rising up to the nostrils of the little unleavened God. We sing our act of submission to his glory.

Tantum ergo Sacramentum
Veneremur cernui:
Et antiquum documentum
Novo cedat ritui ...

Survival was Grandpa's boast. He'd been saved. And I've no doubt, in his own understated way, he thanked the Lord the rest of his days for granting him the unexpected bounty of a long and contented life; for the opportunity to rear his children in peace and security; for his musical talents and the wherewithal to nurture them, and so on. And yet, from another perspective, such salvation could only ever be partial. For one raised under the auspices of eternity, this temporal life—be it as long as Methuselah's and as blessed as Solomon's—is, of necessity, but a shadow of what is to come. And that is why I venture to suggest that, in a more theological sense, and as mortality crept up on him, my grandfather placed less and less store by his privileged status. I think perhaps he even felt that his brothers had stolen a march on him, that they'd secured divine absolution in advance, without having to endure the torments of purgatory. And here was he, the last of the brood, still on guard, lest his grubby soul slip inadvertently into the path of damnation.

Genitori, Genitoque
Laus et jubilatio,
Salus, honor, virtus quoque
Sit et benedictio ...

'Tantum ergo' is my favourite hymn. It's much better than 'Faith of our Fathers' and 'Soul of My Saviour' and 'Come Holy Ghost' and

the rest. I'm already sick of these, their bland predictability, their trite rhymes and sentiments But I can never have enough of 'Tantum ergo'. If a hymn had a shape, all the others would be square. 'Tantum ergo' is snake-like, restless and wriggly, without straight lines. And you've got to come on Sunday night, to benediction, in order to sing it. Nothing else will do, not even High Mass, not even Christmas Day.

My grandfather couldn't prove that his brothers had been saved, of course, but his reason, his compassionate disposition and his faith in a just Creator all encouraged him to believe that a man who had been hauled through the hell of Ypres would not have to endure another roasting before gaining access to eternal life. Worthy is the lamb that was slain. His other brothers, loosed from their mortal coil before attaining the age of sin, would surely have returned directly to their Almighty Father. As for his sister: what better gift could she have offered her Creator than to dedicate the rest of her life to extolling His glory?

In a word, Grandpa knew he was, at bottom, no more than a common sinner. He realised, too, that his longevity was a mixed blessing. The longer a man lived, the longer his soul was bared to temptation; the more he yielded to that temptation, the greater the need for contrition and, ultimately, just penance. Despite his gentle nature, Grandpa's was not some milk-and-water religion: it offered no easy terms to settle his soul's debt. God asked a high price for his forgiveness, and expected payment on demand. Robert had settled his account by return, as it were. For Thomas, the bill was still outstanding and there was no point him haggling over terms. Who would deny the owner of the vineyard the right to reward his servants as he wished? And that was another lesson he learned about the Almighty's code of justice. God's will *would* be done, come what may. He learned this and acceded to it somewhat against the grain, I should think, for he was, as I've said, a man of reason.

Be that as it may, in his later years, and despite this knowledge, Thomas Nesbitt feared neither hell nor purgatory. On the face of things, this was odd. Narrow was the gate that led to eternal life and few passed through it. This is what his faith had taught him. Nothing had been spared, either, in detailing the endless torments inflicted upon the damned. Even the flames of purgatory, it was said, burned more fiercely than all the earth's furnaces put together, because iron was a feeble element and easily smelted, compared with the stubborn stuff of a man's soul. I have no doubt that living under the threat of such sanctions tested many a devout believer: fed their nightmares, even pushed them towards insanity. Not so my grandfather. 'Purgatory? No need to worry about purgatory, child.' He said this with that same mischievous half-smile you can see in the two pictures. The reason for his equanimity was simple: he had discovered a way of drawing purgatory's sting.

As well as being a man of reason, my grandfather also prided himself in his thrift. Grandma was no different. An air of frugality prevailed in their household. They had neither telephone, car nor washing machine; carpets were replaced when threadbare; clothes, as far as I remember, seemed never to be replaced. In my mind's eye, I see my grandfather always in his loose grey suit; my grandmother in her blue floral dress, brooch at the lapel, glinting modestly. They were children of their age; make-do-and-mend was their watchword, reinforced by the penury of their own upbringing.

It was only natural, perhaps, that aspects of this frugality should spill over into Grandpa's religious life. He counted the pennies; he kept an equally watchful eye on his spiritual balance. The church gave him every encouragement to do so. 'Place your credit in the church's treasury,' said the theologians. 'Come the Day of Judgement you may offer it to the Divine Banker, interest and all, a down payment on your eternal life.' Grace was their currency, of course, not money—or, at least, not money alone—but the same principles applied. 'Save your plenty against your want,' they said.

In his old age, my grandfather became a meticulous book-keeper of the soul and took great delight in the observances of that office. Whilst never referring to any specific fall from grace, he spoke with zeal about the prayers and rituals he could employ to ameliorate the consequences of his sinful life. It was as though he had bought a truss for half price and felt compelled to boast his good fortune, despite the unsavoury nature of the object in question and his unwillingness to reveal the condition which required its purchase.

Indulgences were still plentiful in Grandpa's time: indeed, they were the order of the day, along with the Latin, the miracles, the incense and the bleeding hearts. I remember two that he found especially efficacious. One was called Saint Dominic's blessing. This bestowed an indulgence of a hundred days' remission for each Hail Mary. My grandfather, always a keen arithmetician, delighted in telling me that this meant five years if he said the whole rosary. He added that he'd even caught the bus up to St Dominic's in Newcastle, years back, to ask the monks to bless his beads, thinking they'd do it best, they'd be the official purveyors of that saint's beneficence. Then there was the Indulgence of the Cross, which offered *five* hundred days' remittance for every prayer recited. He said how much he regretted not having had wind of this indulgence earlier in life, instead of wasting his time with the Dominicans. And chuckled.

But the *pièce de résistance*, without doubt, was his discovery in old age that he could receive a plenary indulgence—that is, a full reprieve from the tortures of purgatory—simply through listening to the Pope delivering his *Urbi et Orbi* blessing on the radio. He greeted news of this papal favour with some incredulity; and it was, indeed, a remarkable piece of spiritual conjuring that could render fifteen minutes of listening to the wireless equivalent to a pilgrimage to Rome. But that's what it said in *The Universe* and *The Catholic Herald*, and they surely couldn't both be wrong. 'Well I never!' he said. 'What a turn-up!' Once he walked up to our house to see the broadcast on television, figuring, perhaps, that the indulgence would be more surely clinched by means of both sight and sound, rather than through the ears alone. And at that moment, as he crossed himself in acknowledgement of the pontiff's blessing, I swear I could see the grace pouring into his soul. God alone knows for what transgressions he sought absolution. Old lapses, no doubt, from the time of the spats.

'And he cometh to his disciples, and findeth them asleep, and he saith to Peter: What? Could you not watch one hour with me?"

Father Hedley climbs up into the pulpit on the left side of the nave. He has removed his cope and humeral. Stripped down to his cassock and surplice. he is now no better than his altar servers.

'And were the Lord to enter our church today and ask once more, "Could you not watch one hour with me?" what answer would we give? Would we walk with him to the garden to share his torments? To wipe his brow? To offer our prayers and comfort? Mm? Or would we scrub around for some excuse? "No, not tonight, Lord. So sorry, I must go out tonight. Made other arrangements, you see. Old friends. Yes, I promised to call round, don't want to disappoint ..." Is that what we would say?

'Then Jesus approaches his disciples again: "Only an hour," he says. "I ask no more. Will you not spend one hour with me?" How do we respond to this second, even more heartfelt entreaty from our Saviour? "Tomorrow night, my Lord. Tomorrow night would be best. God willing." Is that how we would greet our Saviour? Is that how we would thank him for his sacrifice?'

No-one answers Father Hedley's questions. These are not questions that seek an answer. They are admonishments, merely

dressed up as questions. And I must confess that while Father Hedley
tells his story well enough, with a good sprinkling of dramatic pauses
and pleading hands, I am more than a little irritated by it. I should
sympathise with him, I know, having to dress up and take God out of
his box and intone the litanies, just for a handful of old age
pensioners. But I don't. It's all so unfair. We're not the ones to blame
for leaving Jesus on his own in the garden. It's the fault of the others,
the ones who didn't *come tonight. And I can't understand why we, the*
faithful, have to take the flack for the indifference of those others. 'Go
and give them *a piece of your mind.' That's what I want to say.*
'Take it out on them, *not us.'*

Nor do I like his voice. It's high and whiney. Like a saw cutting
through wood. Back and forth, back and forth. A rusty old saw.

Sins from the days of the spats. That's what my grandfather
was repenting, bound to be. And I've an idea the smile
above the spats means something different to the smile
above the organ. Look at them again, side by side. The
spats smile is a touch more carnal, wouldn't you say? It's the
smile of a man who isn't yet living under the shadow of his
own mortality, even though the sister from Mount Sion is
standing right by him. And it's funny, isn't it, how the
wimple seems to rebuke the spats for their impious
swagger? Even in this monochrome world, some are more
black-and-white than others. But what does he care?

My grandfather was an organist back then, too, in the
1920s. But hymns and voluntaries weren't his sole métier.
He was, you might say, a musical mongrel in his youth. For
every Sunday evening at Sant Cuthbert's, he spent three or
four others down at the Howard Hall, some two hundred
yards away, accompanying Buster Keaton, Charlie Chaplin,
Laurel and Hardy and the other stars of the silent screen.
When it was a religious film on the bill—*Ben-Hur*, say, or
The Ten Commandments—he'd take the choir to sing in the
background, to give the show a proper holy feel.

I wonder, now, what piece Grandpa chose to accompany Moses as he received the tablets? How did he convey the astonishment of the crowd when Jesus cured Ben-Hur's mother of leprosy? Whatever it was, it did the trick. Grandpa got a big clap after every film. Grandma said he had a standing ovation once, which was more than they gave Ramon Novarro or Theodore Roberts. And he went for a pint then, to slake his thirst. He was fond of his pint in the old days, Grandma said, in the age of the spats and the silent films.

'One last time Jesus said, "Come and watch with me and pray that you enter not into temptation ..." And with some urgency in his voice by now, I should think. He knew the hour had come. He knew this would be his last chance to speak with his friends, to warn them of ...'

It won't be a long sermon, I know. The Sunday evening sermon is a mere aside compared with the morning performance. And for that reason I am not surprised, at the outset, to hear Grandpa pulling the stops out. Tock ... Tock ... Tock ... Tock ... Indeed, it seems quite the sensible thing to do, to get the organ primed up for the final hymn. At the same time, I don't recall hearing this before, the plock plock of the stops, right in the middle of the sermon, with Father Hedley in full flow. It's quite an intrusive sound, too, given that there is no other, except the priest's insistent whine. Tock ... Tock ... Tock ... Intrusive enough to make several members of the choir—Dennis, for example, who stands at the end of my own row, and Grandma, of course, who hears everything Grandpa does—turn to see what is afoot.

"And he cometh again and findeth them sleeping: for their eyes were heavy ..."

I'm surprised, too, that he needs to pull out so many stops. It is a powerful organ and we are few, and it can only be for a hymn. A hymn at the wrong time, but still a hymn, because that's all that's left. But then, when the first chord sounds, and it's a single, thunderous, protracted chord, so that the floor trembles beneath my feet, it's clear that this is no ordinary hymn. Then, when I hear the next chord, and the next, the pipes behind me blaring out their strident trebles, their growling bass, I know that this is something I have no name for. Indeed, I begin to wonder whether it is music of any kind, or else a mere cacophony, a fierce, anarchic wrestling between limbs, keys, bellows and pipes. But whatever it is, Grandpa's organ is now in control and Father Hedley's voice is just a pair of pouting lips, a red face, a gaze of sterile indignation. Down there, in your mean little pulpit, you can't touch us. That's what Grandpa's organ says. Do your damndest, little man, I have God's own voice on my side.

Then everyone turns: Dennis again, and Grandma and Mam and Amy and Hilary, and the whole choir. Down in the sanctuary the altar servers look up from their seats. Father Hedley stares. And although his anger is mute, his eyes speak still, telling us, No, this is not how things are meant to be, not in my church.

Mam leans over and whispers. 'Tell him, Anthony, will you?' Because I'm the nearest, so who else? 'Give him a nudge,' she says. 'Go on, quick.' Grandma shakes her head, looks ready to cry. I turn and see Grandpa's feet dancing up and down the pedals, heel-toe, heel-toe; his fingers straddling the chords; his face in the mirror, tight-lipped in concentration. I reach out a hand.

Grandma said she'd never seen such a thing, and he should be ashamed of himself. Mam said it was the mirror's fault, he couldn't see the pulpit and didn't realise that Father Hedley was still preaching. I didn't understand that. There was nothing wrong with Grandpa's hearing and he didn't have to see the pulpit to know that the sermon hadn't finished.

Next Sunday the 'young organist' came to play, both for Mass and Benediction. Grandma said that Grandpa was too embarrassed to show his face. I was glad he didn't come. He would have had to sit downstairs, in the middle of the congregation, and that was no place for Grandpa. His place was up in the gallery, making the floor tremble, showing the priest who was boss. He didn't come the following Sunday either.

A few weeks later I went to see how he was. He said, 'Can you feel them, Anthony?' He bent forward, holding his left ear. 'Just there. Can you feel them?' That's where they were, he said, the wires, growing out of his ear. And if he could only get rid of the wires, things would be alright. He didn't mention the organ at all. Or Father Hedley. Or indulgences. Just the wires.

Eric 'n' Ernie

'What d'you think of it so far?' asks the little one with the hairy legs. 'Rubbish!' says the other.

My father's sitting with his back to the window. His legs are stretched out in front of him, the left foot resting on the right. He is in fact more lying than sitting, and his body fills the chair. From here he can watch the television without turning his head; he can see me, too, with only the slightest shift of his eyes.

'Absolute rubbish!' says the tall one with the spectacles. 'Ha!'

Dad laughs. A little cough of a laugh. He rearranges his legs, rests the right foot on the left, gives his nose a rub with the knuckle of his index finger. This is his favourite programme and he is in a good mood. 'Ha!' He folds his hands across his belly, across his grey cardigan.

I am sitting at the far end of the sofa, which stands a little to the left of my father's chair. Because of this arrangement I must turn my head in order to see the screen, and turn it at least a quarter revolution in the opposite direction to see my father's face. But I rarely do this unless he is speaking to me. His grey socks and black trousers, however, are in full view. Through the corner of my eye, just past the thick frame of my spectacles, I see a rough outline of the rest of his body.

In the angle between my father's chair and the sofa stands a small oblong table. This is where my mother has left our supper. Sandwiches of some kind, I'm not sure what. She's covered them with plastic bowls so that they don't dry out. And a little cake each, too, under their own white bowl. That's the routine. Shortly my father will get up and go to the kitchen to make a pot of tea for himself. Because if Mam made the tea before she went out it wouldn't be fit to drink come suppertime. 'And what would your dad say then?'

Mam's gone to see her old friend, Peggy. Once a month they meet up, and have done so since before I can remember. Which is not long, as I'm only fifteen years of age. I like Peggy. She tells funny stories about the Land Army during the war and about meeting her husband there. Her husband's name is Bob and he's in Morpeth, which means that he's not right in his head, but you've got to say that under your breath, so nobody else hears. Mam goes to see Bob as well sometimes. 'I'm away to see Bob,' she says, not 'I'm away to Morpeth.' This is a phrase to be used with care. 'She's off to Morpeth, is she?' No, you wouldn't use such a phrase lightly.

It strikes eight. It's suppertime and my father has made his tea. No-one says anything, but that is the routine in our house. Eight o'clock, suppertime. And although it would be easier for me to get at my food if I sat at the other end of the sofa, next to the table, this is not what I do. Even though I could quite comfortably perch there for a few seconds, to collect my plate, and then return to my original position, I eschew this option as well. It would, I think, be a strange and unnerving act, to move closer to my father only to retreat then into my private little recess. So I stay where I am, at the far end of the sofa. As a result, there is a gap between me and my father, the gap where Mam would normally sit. In order to respect that gap I must get up and approach the table from behind the sofa. This is what I do. As soon as I've fetched my plate of sandwiches I return to my seat.

My father's routine is different. First, he tucks his napkin into his shirt collar. Then, leaning over the arm of his chair, he lifts the plastic cover from his plate. The sandwiches have already been cut into neat quarters. He proceeds to open each one and dab a little mustard on the meat. Why didn't Mam do this before she went out? I don't know. I can only surmise that they've had a row about it at some point: a row I missed because I was at school at the time or playing football with my friends. 'You always put too much mustard on my sandwiches, woman!' Or, alternatively: 'You never put enough mustard on my sandwiches, woman. I might as well do it myself!' Something to that effect. And go off in a sulk. Anyway, it's meat sandwiches my father's got. Mine are cheese and chutney. These have been cut into little quarters, too, but there's no need to add mustard. I hate mustard.

'You can't see the join,' declares the tall one, the one with the glasses, as he examines the head of his friend, the short one with hairy legs.

Having got his sandwiches ready, my father leans over the arm of his chair once more and loops his fingers around the handle of the teapot. The teapot is wrapped in a woolly jacket, knitted in brown, blue and red stripes, with a little woolly ball on top. Grandma made this. Grandma made the antimacassars on the chairs, too, but it was Mam who made the napkins and embroidered the little purple flowers on them. Dad is pouring his tea. He always pours the tea first. That is his routine. After setting the teapot back down on the table, he reaches for the milk jug. I see these things through the corner of my eye. The yellow jug. The fingers opening, seeking the handle.

Eric Morecombe has a paper bag in his right hand. What is he holding in his left hand? I can't see anything. Whatever it is, this thing I can't see, he throws it into the air. And although Ernie can't see anything either, his eyes follow it, this invisible thing, all the way up and all the way down, until it falls into the bag. Plock! The sound makes me think it must be a stone or a marble or perhaps a little rubber ball. Eric throws it again. Their eyes follow again, all the way up and all the way down. Plock! It is only on seeing the trick for the third time that I realise that there is nothing there, neither stone nor rubber ball, that this is nothing but illusion. What, then, makes the sound? I cannot tell.

As Eric throws the invisible ball a fourth time, my dad draws his fingers back from the milk jug. Without altering his posture—his body is still half turned towards the little table—he pulls both hands to his stomach and winces. I see this, all in a brief glance, moving only my eyes: my face still watches the television. I have half a sandwich in my hand. I have crossed my legs and am holding the plate quite close to my mouth now, in case of crumbs. I change none of these things. And although I cannot see my father very well —the frame of my spectacles is in the way—I can make out the redness in his face, the eyes tight shut. Plock! The ball falls into the bag once more.

It's Ernie's turn to have a go. He takes hold of the invisible ball and throws it into the air, just as Eric did before him. Nothing happens. Everyone is primed to hear the Plock! At the same time, we all know that it won't happen, because it's Eric who's still holding the bag. This is Eric's game. Dad moans, quietly to begin with, just a little whimper from somewhere down in his throat. 'Nn.' As though something has got stuck there. 'Nn.' Ernie stares at the bag. Then he looks up above him and wonders whether the invisible ball has perhaps become lodged in the curtains, or in the lights, or maybe one of the stage hands has caught it, out of devilment. 'Oof.' Dad's whimper turns into a groan. His breathing speeds up. Like an old bellows. Like a pig. Like I don't know what. Speeds up, becomes phlegmy, more nasal. Like a donkey. And that, too, is part of the routine.

When this happened before, Mam knew what to do. She phoned the doctor. And even though the doctor was a woman, and Mam paid heavily for her mistake, this was certainly the correct procedure. But Mam isn't here now. And you might imagine that I would do the same thing, following her example. Phone the doctor. Or the ambulance, perhaps, bearing in mind the time of night. Describe the symptoms. Give our address. That sort of thing. And all would be sorted. My father would be someone else's responsibility and no-one here need take the blame for anything. Yes, that is what you'd expect. But how can I do such a thing? How can I possibly phone for an ambulance without my dad's permission? 'Would you like an ambulance, Dad? Would you like to go to the hospital? Where's the pain exactly?' No, I don't dare. And in any case, I doubt whether he is in a fit state to understand, let alone answer, such questions. So I say nothing of doctors or hospitals or symptoms or anything of the kind. Do I say something else, then, if only to fill the gap, to respond in some way to the groaning by my side? Can I fetch you something, Dad? Water? Aspirin? Milk of Magnesia? No, I do not. I watch the television.

Eric is now juggling with the invisible ball. It is definitely a ball, I can see that now. I mean, it is without doubt the illusion of a ball. He heads it, he bounces it on his shoulders, he balances it on his foot just like a professional footballer and flicks it back onto his head. I watch these things intently. I watch them in order not to watch my father. The temptation to snatch just one sly glance is almost impossible to suppress. But that is what I must do. My father hates being watched. So, I watch the television. Despite this, I no longer hear any of the dialogue, and that's a pity. This is clearly a very funny sketch, the audience is roaring with laughter. I hear scarcely a word because my father is making too much noise. You might say that, if he was merely groaning before, and then, little by little, started making pig noises and then donkey noises, he is now roaring like a bull. I exaggerate, of course, but I am only fifteen years of age, these are the images, the words, that come to mind, and how else can I describe such unpleasant sensations?

Ernie has had enough of his friend's antics. He takes the bag from Eric's hand, scrunches it up and throws it into the middle of the audience. Eric stares at him, wide-eyed, shocked, and then at the audience. At me. He pulls a face, the famous face that says, 'I have been wronged, my friends. Come, feel my sorrow, my hurt.' He undoes that hurt by starting a new game, by making a game of the wrong itself.

'Can I have my ball back, please?' says Eric. The audience laughs again. We all know that Eric can't be beaten now, that the silly little man with the hairy legs has already yielded victory, merely by trying to fight back. I don't have to hear the words to understand this: the meaning is all in the gestures: Ernie, chastising his friend, then smiling that cold, formal, self-righteous smile of his, trying to enlist our sympathy, failing utterly; Eric, with his bruised, confused, hang-dog look, as he straightens his tie, adjusts his spectacles. Yes, he has been wronged. But he will be the victor.

My father sits forward in his chair, his hands wrapped tightly around his abdomen. I can see his head clearly now. I can see the bald patch on his crown, and his shirt collar, which has runkled up on one side so that it almost touches his ear. It's an old blue shirt from his police days. Perhaps he hasn't attached the collar properly. Perhaps he's lost the knack. The groaning and bellowing have stopped. In their place I hear only a delicate little 'Ts, ts', between the teeth, the odd 'Dear, dear'.

This, too, is part of the routine. And for that reason I am not overly concerned. Don't misunderstand me. Witnessing such a performance makes me feel uneasy. I should prefer to be elsewhere. I should even prefer to be in my bedroom, if that were possible, but retreating to one's bedroom other than to sleep has not yet become common practice amongst teenagers and the possibility does not cross my mind. But I am not insensitive. As I say,

I feel uneasy. I feel the distress of a fifteen-year-old boy whose father has suddenly started to behave inappropriately.

Eric, having enlisted our sympathy, reaches into his jacket pocket and pulls out another bag. The audience roars its approval that the nice big man is about to outwit the unpleasant little man once again. And nobody minds that Ernie snatches this bag, too, scrunches it into a ball and tosses it over his shoulder, because Eric has an inexhaustible store of them: up his shirt sleeves, in his trouser pockets, down the side of his shoe. No-one minds, then, that Ernie—the ever rational Ernie—sets about stripping Eric, frisking him, doing everything in his power to expel the evil genie and restore law and order. No-one minds in the slightest. We know that Eric has won. That he has won from the very beginning.

My father must have leaned further forward without me noticing because he suddenly slips to the floor. No, slips is the wrong word. Slips suggests a certain smoothness of movement, and something quite discrete, without too much commotion. But he doesn't fall, either. Fall implies loss of control. This is a deliberate act, I have no doubt of it. So, he lowers himself onto his knees. Lowers? It will have to do. Despite this being a deliberate, premeditated act, however, the two knees strike the floor with a *bump!* that makes me start. I have not witnessed this manoeuvre before. It is not part of the normal sequence of events. There is another reason, too, why I am disconcerted. Through the thick twill of my father's trousers, and in spite of the plush fireside rug beneath him, I hear his bones click and crunch. And it is a strange thing to say, I know, but until tonight I did not realise—I did not fully *appreciate*— that my father possessed bones. *Bump!* The sound is louder than you might expect, too, but you must remember that he is on the heavy side—seventeen stone, according to my mother—and his knees hit the floor before he has a chance to put out his hands and spread the weight. The knees, therefore, bear the full impact. Seventeen stone.

But he is not to be daunted. Having splayed his hands flat on the floor, he steadies himself, takes a deep breath. 'Fffff ...' And another. 'Fffff ...' As if to say, 'Well, that's better, after all that malarkey, yes, a lot better, to be down here, on my hands and knees, having a bit of a breather.' And for a while he seems more composed, less troubled. So that I wonder, was this all part of the plan? Has he done it before? Did I miss something else when I was at school, or playing football? I shall have to ask Mam when she gets home. Anyway, there's nothing for it now but to stay where he is, at least for a moment, on all fours, to gather his thoughts, to plan what to do next. He takes another deep breath. 'Fffff.' And another. 'Fffff.' Which is almost a sigh. A sigh of relief.

Dad's napkin is on the floor. It has fallen out of his collar which, as I say, was not properly buttoned and therefore provided little purchase. I realise, of course, that Dad has other things on his mind at the moment, but dear knows, he needs a napkin. Because here, on his hands and knees, his face to the floor, and with all that puffing and panting, he has begun to drivel copiously. And a son should not have to witness his father doing such things.

Ought I pick up the napkin and give it back to him? I consider this question for a moment. The answer is 'No', and a clear, resounding 'No' at that. For one thing, Dad would not be able to use the napkin at present. His hands are on the floor, bearing his whole weight, so I'm sure he could not pick it up, let alone raise it to his mouth. Secondly, the act of offering a napkin to my father, under current circumstances, would certainly be misinterpreted. As though I were poking fun at him. 'Your belly's about to burst, Dad? Well, here you are. Here's a napkin for you.' And in any case, it is not fitting for a fifteen year old boy to lean over a man twice his size, to look down upon him in his distress, to proffer his clumsy, juvenile parody of succour. I refrain. It is best.

No, Eric is not to be beaten. He joins in the game—the spiteful little game that Ernie initiated—finding ever more paper bags, in his socks, in his braces, even in Ernie's own jacket. (A brilliant touch, this.) Everyone laughs. Everyone except Ernie, Dad and me. It would not be seemly for me to laugh, however funny the sketch. And I would, of course, have turned the television off, given half a chance. I mean, given permission. Because it is the television, with its raucous laughter and gusto, that causes me the greatest unease. Even a boy of my tender years, with little experience of the world and its ways, knows instinctively that such fripperies are not compatible with watching his father crawl on his hands and knees, bellowing his distress. But this is his favourite programme. And who's to say, beneath all that groaning and panting, behind those red cheeks and watery eyes, that my father is not himself having a hearty chuckle at the two clowns and their pranks?

Yes, crawling on his hands and knees. That's what he's doing now. Crawling. And I must pull my feet in, as far as I can, to allow him to pass. I'm not surprised that he's started to crawl. The fire is alight—it's mid-October and the evenings are getting chilly—and no-one could stay there for long, so close to the flames. These are little gas fire flames, of course, not the coal flames of yesteryear. But heat is heat. Two veins stand out on his temple, as though they too were ready to burst.

Step by little step, Dad goes on his way, the right leg first, then the right hand; the left leg, then the left hand. As is only natural, I suppose, for a man who is intent on crawling. After every four steps or so, he pauses for a while, to get his wind back. And I'm not sure, on reflection, whether 'step' is the correct term for movements of this kind. It doesn't sound right, somehow, but I can't for the life of me think of another. Which is strange, given that we all, each and every one of us, must crawl at some time or other in our lives. Anyway, with the third sequence of steps —leg, hand, leg, hand—he has safely passed the fire and I am beginning to wonder whether he is making a beeline for the television: to change the channel, perhaps, even to switch it off. Neither is likely, I admit. Why would Dad change channels in the middle of his favourite programme? I am fairly certain, too, that he would not crave complete silence under the current circumstances. It is much better, for both Dad and me, that there is a little background noise. True, it is not enough to drown out the groaning and bellowing. It scarcely masks the panting. But it is better than nothing.

Singers from Cuba are performing now. And I think, yes, perhaps music is better than comedy for circumstances such as these. It is, for one thing, more fitting, less incongruous, as a background to pain and its noisier symptoms. It also suffers fewer interruptions—there are none of the little gaps you get in even the funniest sketches —so it offers a more continuous barrier to those unwelcome noises. As I say, singers from Cuba. *Los* something or other. Clicking their fingers, shaking their hips, smiling through their white teeth. A sunny, cheerful song, full of sweet harmonies and jaunty syncopations. But Dad passes the television by without so much as a glance. His whole body is in view now, and for a few seconds I am able to scrutinise it without fear: from his grey socks to his hunched shoulders. But for a few seconds only because, having crawled past the television, having gone around the other chair between the sofa and the wall, he disappears from view. And yet, although I cannot see him now, I am fairly sure, judging by the noises I hear, that he is doing exactly as before. Right leg, right hand, left leg, left hand, and then a little pause. 'Oof, oof.' Right leg, right hand, left leg, left hand. 'Oof.'

Where are you going, Dad? Where on earth are you going? Surely you're not going to the bathroom? Yes. He's trying to get to the bathroom. Of course he is. His belly is about to burst and he needs to go to the toilet. Or else fetch the Milk of Magnesia. And if only I'd asked earlier, when I thought about these things for the first time, I could have saved him a lot of trouble, and I would not now be in such a quandary. Can I fetch you something, Dad? Water? Aspirin? Milk of Magnesia? If only I'd asked sooner.

Yes, he's going to the bathroom.

And on my life, I haven't the foggiest idea how he'll do it. Can a man climb the stairs on all fours? Can Dad drag his seventeen stone, step by step, from the bottom to the top? Right leg, right hand, left leg, left hand. Is such a thing possible? And after all that trouble, that effort, would he then arrive in time? Because he's been at it already for a good five minutes and he's barely reached the far end of the sitting room. And down, then, of course. He'd surely want to come down again, to catch the end of the programme. How would he do that? On his backside? I feel a sudden urge to get up, to offer him a helping hand. To open the door, perhaps. Although that, too, of course, would entail leaning over my father and I'm not sure I'm capable of such a thing, however pressing the need. Even if I were wholly convinced, in principle, that this was the right thing to do, I doubt whether I could muster the courage, the presumption, to carry it out. I'm sure my father would agree. 'You cheeky young monkey.' That's what he'd say. Something like that. I can hear his voice now, in my head.

But he's still crawling. He's passed the television. And he's passed the door, too. I can hear him behind the sofa now, puffing and panting, moaning and groaning. And it is, I admit, unpleasant and more than a little disturbing to hear my father making such noises behind my back, when I can do nothing about it, when I cannot even turn to check on his progress. I'm put in mind of the game my brother and I used to play, when we were little. He'd hide behind the sofa and jump out to frighten me. Pretend to be a wolf, a lion, a bear, come to tear me limb from limb. But Dad isn't a wolf. He's more like a dog. An old, lame dog, panting behind the sofa, his tongue hanging out over his wet lips. Drivelling on the floor. 'Oof. Oof.'

Eric returns to the stage, carrying a guitar. He pretends to sing some Latin American song. The words are all in cod Spanish, the melody is full of fancy turns and trills. Both voice and guitar are excrutiatingly out of tune. Ernie puts his hands over his ears, winces. But Eric continues to sing with gusto. I look at the *Radio Times* to see what else is on this evening. This programme is due to end in two minutes and we need to decide what to watch next. What would Dad like? I don't think he's in any fit state to speak for himself. Not yet, anyway. So I must guess, and guess correctly. Mam will be back in an hour. An hour and a half, perhaps. I've got a stitch. The cheese sandwich has given me indigestion. It's too soon to go to bed.

Speaking in Tongues

'Mam.'

Your mother tongue takes you as close to truth as language will allow. You soon learn the art of deception, but that's a different matter. Whatever lies you peddle, the elemental core remains. It stays there, tucked in under the ribs, with the heart and guts. It speaks the body, not just the mind. A second language is a lie from the outset. However truthful the words you haltingly scramble together, it never settles into the bloodstream, the muscle tissue. To get by in that borrowed medium, to make *yourself* plausible, you must don a mask and embark on the art of mimicry. You must try to *act* what you cannot *be*. At best your second language becomes a well disguised, mechanically adroit prosthetic.

Yes, at best. Acquiring a second language is all well and good if you have the necessary attributes. But these are numerous and complex. A good memory for vocabulary and grammar is merely a starting point: it allows the production of a script, but not its performance. Mimicry demands not only the ability to learn quickly and to recall unhesitatingly (or, if hesitating, to do so idiomatically), it also requires the whole body to follow suit: the tongue, to trill subtle melodies quite alien to its natural habitat; the hands, the tilt of the head, the shrugging shoulders, and so on, to give mere words the weight of flesh and bone.

These are hard lessons, not lightly undertaken and only painstakingly learned. Nevertheless, students of French will, through a period of immersion, achieve a good enough approximation to the real thing to make themselves understood and, perhaps, even embraced in their adopted tongue. This is because your French interlocutor is likely to be as faltering in English as you are in their language. The same goes for Spanish, Russian, Mandarin, and so on. Your predicament is shared and understood. Above all, the need to communicate wins out over your mutual discomfort.

A brief example. Once, with the residue of my O-level French, I entered a Montmartre *fromagerie* to buy a slice of cheese. The vendor, eager to please, but lacking English, had to collaborate in my struggle. She tolerated my errors, proffered alternatives for me to consider, knowing there was no option but silence and failure. 'Quatre grammes, monsieur? C'est tout? Vous êtes sûr?' I took my transparent sliver of cheese, affected a bluff nonchalance. 'Merci. Un petit morceau. C'est bon.' A hard lesson, but my French was the better for it. Making a fool of myself was par for the course: a necessary stage on the path to fluency and acceptance.

Those trying to learn Welsh have a harder time of it, and this has nothing to do with the language itself. Having hunted around for some time to locate your Welsh-speaking grocer, you launch your 'Llaeth ...?' into the unforgiving air. That single word—too much drawn out, or else a touch too clipped; pronounced with too northern an inflection, or perhaps too southern—is enough to elicit a hearty 'Learning Welsh are you? Jolly good ... Now, is it skimmed or semi-skimmed?' Next time you make sure to say 'Lla'th', or 'Llefrith', as the case may be. You even hedge it about with greetings and asides in a scrupulously brushed-up vernacular. But it's too late. Your secret's out, the imposter has been unmasked. And basically they've got better things to do than be your unpaid tutor. You both know that milk is milk. All else is so much froth.

This was all clear to me within a week of starting college. I had worked diligently over the summer holidays to prepare myself for the imminent move. *Teach Yourself Welsh* had been my bedtime reading. Lunchtime Welsh-language broadcasts, aimed at the diaspora, had helped me atune my ear (or so I believed) to what I would shortly encounter in the flesh. Alas, during that very first week, I discovered that neither a rote-learned pluperfect of the verb 'bwyta' nor the eloquent disquisitions of T. H. Parry-Williams equipped me for my encounters with Cardiganshire shopkeepers. 'Duw, there's deep Welsh you've got ... Carrots was it?' Not only was I conspicuously English and lacking in fluency, I was also a pretentious upstart. 'Yes, carrots, please.' I retreated, a rootless vegetable.

It would have been easier, of course—or so I convinced myself—if my English had had a Welsh accent. I might then have appealed to a wider sense of commonality, eased myself into a position of trust and slipped, phrase by phrase, mutation by mutation, into the vernacular. I was, I thought, too much in my tongue. In fact, I realised that to all intents and purposes, I *was* my tongue. I even came to envy, in an idle and facile way, the victims of that strange condition, Foreign Accent Syndrome. I had read about the case of the Norwegian woman who, having suffered a head injury during World War II, thereafter spoke her native language with a strong German accent, although the German language was utterly unknown to her and she had never visited Germany. Her Norwegian even displayed many of the distortions and idiosyncracies that characterise second-language speakers. Of course, I did not desire her fate: neither the shrapnel, nor the fact that she was then ostracised by her community. What I sought was not the transformation itself, but the *semblance* of that transformation. Somehow, if I was to learn Welsh, I had to divest myself of my Englishness.

My strategy was a radical and, I think, original one. Now, it is impossible simply *not* to be English. To do so would mean becoming a mere absence, a person shorn of history and attributes. Such an endeavour is, I believe, unsustainable. In order not to be English, one must become something else. I decided to become Italian. It was an obvious choice. I had my name on my side, an irrefutable piece of evidence, inscribed on my passport, my Students Union card, my cheque book, for all the world to see. I would make it work for me.

So far so good. The next step was to billet myself somewhere remote, where no-one knew me, where I could nurture my new Italian self in some modicum of security. Before my second term began, and in face of stern opposition from the college authorities ('Who will take your room?' 'How will you travel back and forth?' etc.) I moved out of my hall of residence and rented a two-roomed cottage in a village some eleven miles away. (In those days such cottages could be had for as little as £3 a week.) The village boasted a shop, a pub, two chapels, a small primary school and, on its outskirts, a warehouse stocking fertiliser, animal feed and the like. The college had been right, of course: it would be difficult for me to come and go; in fact, given the infrequent bus service, it would be quite impossible to attend any lectures before eleven o'clock. But this was the price I had to pay for my seclusion. Such was the village's remoteness and inconvenience, no other student would dream of taking lodgings there. Besides, I already knew that few attended lectures before eleven o'clock wherever they were billeted. The cottage's name was Ty'n-y-bedw, although, as far as I could see, no beech trees grew in the vicinity.

Before moving in I went on a modest shopping spree at the second-hand clothes stall in Carmarthen market. I'd seen Fellini's *8½* at the college film club and it had made me painfully aware of the incongruity of my clothes: an amalgam of Bri-nylon t-shirts, indestructible and shapeless Terylene trousers, and a tweed jacket for best. Knowing little Italian and displaying few ancestral features, I needed at least to look the part. Had I followed my peers in the direction of flares and tie-dyes I might have struck a more international posture, but parental disapproval, as well as personal inertia, had closed off experimentation in that arena.

There were few Italian labels on show at Carmarthen market. Nevertheless, I found a handsome powder-blue jacket that pulled in nicely at the waste when buttoned and squared off my shoulders more severely than if I'd left the hanger in place. I also bought a blue-and-white striped shirt, a pair of light grey trousers with a crease that would have sliced bread, and some brown brogues. The result might not have been strictly Italian but it was—to my mind, at least—a great deal less English. Back in the village, I presented myself to the locals as an Italian exchange student, dedicated to learning Welsh and fostering mutual understanding between our peoples, etc. A young Welsh woman ('from Llannerch-y-medd, you won't know her ...') was reciprocating at the University of Pavia.

'That's £9.50 for the month,' the owner said. 'Month in advance.' He was called Wil, wore a cap and spoke very fast with minimal abduction of the jaw or parting of the lips. I said, 'Quando?' And paused. Then, 'Non parlo molto d'Inglese.' And then, 'Dim Saesneg.' I tried to give my Welsh a little Italian twist.

Wil lifted the peak of his cap and looked up at me. He considered the cut of my jacket and trousers.

'No English?'

I took out my Students' Union membership card and pointed to my name; or, at least, to my surname. I covered my Christian name with my thumb. 'Veno de l'Italia. Parlo Italiano. Dim Saesneg. Italiano e Cymraeg.'

'Cwmrâg?'

'Si ... Ie.'

'Dim Saesneg?'

'Un pò. Solo un pò. Tipyn bach.'

By that evening, when I met Wil in the Farmer's Arms, he had already told his friends about the strange student staying at Ty'n-y-bedw who had no English and wore clothes a size too small for him. They greeted me with bashful smiles. I recognised the shopkeeper, who sported the full sideburns of the previous decade. The others I assumed to be farmers and were unknown to me. For a while they remained mute. I had learned that Welsh in these parts was spoken either very fast or not at all. Wil and his friends had decided, rightly enough, that fast would be beyond my comprehension, so they opted, for a while, for not at all. This suited me well enough. I offered my set pieces—I'd been practising them for several days in expectation of this or some similar occasion—and demanded of them no more than an occasional nod or shake of the head, a brief 'Wel, wel ...' or 'Ife, wir?' Before the end of my pint, my leaden comments on the weather, on the abundance of crows, on my surprise at the absence of beech trees, had begun to elicit some tentative questions. These were channelled, in the main, through Wil, who in their eyes had become a seasoned interpreter. Had I come far? Did I follow Italian football? (The national team was hotly tipped for the 1970 World Cup.) Anticipating that this might crop up, I had prepared a short paean, in Welsh, to Gigi Riva.

Courteous to a fault, Wil and his friends did not pry into my personal life. I did, nevertheless, present a brief biography of myself, knowing that this, too, would be broadcast in the neighbourhood and help reinforce my new credentials. When my Welsh started fraying at the edges, which was soon enough, I coddled myself in my own assumed vernacular. 'A, e molto difficile ...' When that, too, was all spent—and I had, in truth, only a handful of Italian phrases at my disposal—I resorted to church Latin. 'Domine son sum dignus ... Credo in unum deum ...' I gave it a secular sheen, as best I could, waving my hands about, jerking my head this way and that. My drinking partners didn't seem ruffled. Their nonconformist ears were no doubt impervious to foreign pieties, however delivered.

I visited the shop the following day. It was the sideburns' wife that served me, but she had been well briefed and even greeted me with a cheery 'buon giorno', which wrong-footed me rather. I replied in kind, then switched to Welsh. She graciously followed suit. She and the sideburns had honeymooned in Sorrento, she said. Had I been to Sorrento? Alas, no, I said. I was an orphan. 'Un povero orfano. Plentyn ... mm ... plentyn amddifad?' And we were not afforded such luxuries. I had amplified my biography in this way, not to solicit sympathy but merely as a means of forestalling questions. An orphan had, I supposed, less history to be scrutinised and, perhaps, found wanting. I was relieved that the range of goods in the shop was narrow: it kept my linguistic ambitions in check and my visit short. I left with a pint of milk, a bar of chocolate and a bottle of washing-up liquid. Sqeezy was the only word of English to pass between us. 'Ciao!' she said. 'Hwyl fawr!' I replied.

During the next two months my life in the village established a predictable routine. I greeted my neighbours, and they greeted me, with that slowly gathering access of ease and mutual regard that is the product of settled custom. I drank a late pint at the Farmer's Arms twice a week and built up my Welsh vocabulary, especially in the chief topics of the season: animal gynaecology and the weather. (A severe late cold snap had left deep drifts of snow in the fields above Ty'n-y-bedw.) I shopped, frugally, at the local store. There, notably on pension day, I enjoyed more varied and less arcane discourse, and improved my grasp of idiom and cadence. In little segments such as these my competence gradually increased; my prosthetic started to grow, if not bones and sinew, then at least a plausible epidermis.

This is not to say that, with the waxing of my Welsh, I let my Italian wane. I knew that the integrity of my Italian mask was a prerequisite for the construction of its Welsh equivalent. Indeed, the more I ventured into unfamiliar territory the more I had to buff my inarticulacy with reminders that this stemmed from my foreignness, that is, my non-English foreignness. I broadened my repertoire of catchphrases, peppered my speech with 'mi scusis', 'per favores', 'grazies', 'pregos' and the like. Remembering that showing is always more effective than telling, I then tracked down Bruno Munari's *Speak Italian: the Fine Art of the Gesture.* I followed its detailed diagrams until my gesticulations—hitherto quite random and improvised—acquired some semblance of authenticity. 'Perfetto!' I said, complimenting a neighbour's well-trimmed hedge. 'Perffaith!' And traced an imaginary line with finger and thumb, just as though I were pulling a thread of cotton. When sampling a piece of local cheese, or a new ale at the Farmer's Arms, I would offer a sensual 'mm', make circles in the air with my index finger, then press it into my cheek. 'Buono. Da iawn, wir!' I might add that no-one was more surprised by this gesture than myself, but Signore Munari's diagrams were quite specific and unambiguous. In any case, I knew that my neighbours would be none the wiser. I'm sure I saw the sideburns do it himself on one occasion, drinking his mid-morning cuppa in the shop, nibbling a Welsh cake, poking a finger into his cheek. My Italian ways were catching.

Perhaps I succeeded too well, or at least I stretched the fabric of my new hybridity beyond what its delicate weave would easily sustain. I should have settled for a term at Ty'n-y-bedw then called it a day, moved on, faced up to my demons, the town's grocers and the rest. But no, I signed up for another three months. The summer holidays would soon follow, I could return home and then, come the autumn, slip back into the obscurity of a hall of residence. Such were the thoughts I conjured in order to console myself. Or maybe, there again, that is all just so much persiflage. I think, in fact, I had become a little too attached to my assumed persona. Stretched or not, its fabric was now familiar, recognised, acknowledged: an absurd little home-from-home.

Then, one night in the pub, the sideburns told me that his wife wanted to see Sorrento again. After such a hard winter, she'd said. And more than likely a dismal, wet summer to follow. She, in turn, behind her shop counter, spoke excitedly at the prospect. 'A second honeymoon,' she said. Then, a week later, quite tentatively, 'Would you ...? Do you think you could ...?' She wanted coaching in Italian, the better to enjoy her stay. I should have guessed. She had for some days been handing me little morsels of Italian with my groceries: a 'pane' here, a 'latte' there. It was all building up to this. Perhaps I encouraged her. A blithe, devil-may-care demeanour was, after all, part of my armoury. Anyway, I pointed out, trying to conceal my panic, that she'd had no Italian on her first visit. 'Ah! Young love,' she said. 'Who needs language when they're in love?' I blushed. She persevered. She even offered to pay. 'Well,' I said. I hadn't had to refuse a request of this kind before in Welsh and was unsure of the correct protocol and register. It would have been difficult enough in English. I could, of course, have given her a pertinent gesture from Munari's manual. A wagging index finger, accompanied by a stern 'Niente da fare', would have left an Italian in no doubt. But I judged it too curt for this occasion. I said what came first to mind. 'You see, my Italian is of the mountains ... Eidaleg y mynyddoedd, the mountains of Lombardy ... The Italian of Sorrento is like ... It's like ...' I scrambled for a comparison. 'They're like Pembrokeshire and Anglesey,' I exclaimed, wide-eyed, inviting her awe.

'But at school. You must have learned ...?'

'Yr ysgol? La scuola? Ah, well ...'

This was a question to which I had no answer.

How far do you persevere on your chosen path? What do you do when it becomes intolerably stony or muddy, when it teeters on the edge of a cliff? Is it better to hold your nerve than to retreat and select a new *terra incognito* that might be even worse? How can you possibly know? I thought of the Norwegian woman again, her tongue transplanted at the root without losing a drop of blood. Perhaps, I thought, I could follow her example in a more literal sense than I had dared. I could retreat from the scene for a brief while, then return, somewhat disorientated and distressed, to explain that I had fallen victim to a strange but well-attested neurological event—nothing too serious, although quite dramatic in its fall-out—which had deleted all Italian from my memory, so that I could no longer remember or pronounce a single syllable. I'd have quoted other cases, to give my account weight and credibility. The charade would then have come to an end, or at least been replaced by a lesser fabrication. They might say, 'He's really Italian, you know. You'd never guess, would you? Some illness or other.' But my tongue would no longer have to worry itself. It could trip and skip as it wished. Neurology would have let it off the hook. I pondered the Norwegian woman again, lost to herself and all around her. Could I really affect such a desperate alteration?

In the event, I took the bus to Carmarthen and spent more than I could afford on one of the new-fangled mini cassette recorders—a Phillips, I think. (I remember the little round logo with the waves and stars in it.) I ordered a six-part Colloquial Italian for Beginners course through the post. I started at the beginning. *Mi dispiace ... Non capisco ... Dov'è la toilette?* I recorded my efforts and played them back, checking the intonation, repeating as necessary. I wondered whether I should give the phrases a Lombardian inflection. I wondered what such a thing might be. A lilt, perhaps? An idiosyncratic 'r'? Why did I wonder such things? You might well ask. I think I feared that my pupil would say: 'But that's not how *you* would say it, is it? Say it as *you* would say it, in the mountains of Lombardy. Go on, let me hear you.'

I stayed up until the early hours, sat in the quiet of Ty'n-y-bedw, wondering what tomorrow might bring A return home? A neurological event? A massive erasure? Or perhaps just Lesson Two. Keep one step ahead. *Mi dispiace ... Non capisco ...* And how could that possibly be enough? So Lesson Three as well. And all the others, in turn. And after the lessons were finished, after all the phrases were learned, what then? 'Please, tell me how it was in that orphanage. Please tell me, what will you do when you return? And please, please, what do you Italian men say to women when you ... you know ...?'

So, a return home, a neurological event, a massive erasure. Once and for all. But what was there to erase? And how would I mimic that loss? A mask on top of a mask. I sat in the quiet of Ty'n-y-bedw, following my reflection in the window, still black as pitch although dawn was close. *Mi dispiace ... Mae'n wir ddrwg gen i ... I'm so sorry.*

Black Spot

Only the chapels had real organs: instruments with two keyboards for the hands and another for the feet, and stout women in twin-sets and pudding hats to play them. They presided imperiously above the pulpit and the *sêt fawr*, their pipes rising straight to the heavens, like trumpets of Zion, making sure that God didn't miss a note. Ministers traded in words, but everyone knew that an organ's vibrato was the quiver of the soul. Organists shared something of their instruments' hauteur and mystique. The mother of my girlfriend, Delyth, was one such. And although her chapel stood on the fringes of town and was of a more liberal, unorthodox persuasion than the others, Zion breathed through her pipes, too.

My own church, the Catholic church, for all its claims to pre-eminence, had to make do with a harmonium. This stood on the floor of the nave, pushed up against the wall, as though we were ashamed to call it our own. Whereas the organ was an integral and commanding feature of nonconformist architecture, this instrument was clearly an afterthought, a cheap and incongruous accessory. Bought for twenty pounds in a furniture sale, it never warmed to its new home. I think it missed its previous habitation, wherever that had been: a cosy, carpeted parlour, perhaps; or else some remote mountain sanctuary, where it had got used to the peace and quiet. Maybe it just begrudged being bullied out of retirement. It was a protestant instrument, of that I had no doubt.

In the absence of a twin-setted, pudding-hatted candidate, the job was offered to me, on the strength of my modest abilities as a pianist. I struggled. Whereas a reasonable dexterity of the fingers was sufficient to get by on the piano, the harmonium demanded, in addition, the servitude of feet and legs. It was a hard and pitiless taskmaster. I had to pedal like a man possessed to keep the bare minimum of air in the bellows. Three verses of 'Angels from the Realms of Glory', or one of the other more rumbustious numbers, were enough to leave me as breathless as my instrument. In warm weather, I perspired copiously, adding a film of slipperiness to an already treacherous and recalcitrant keyboard. And although neither of us—myself nor my instrument—counted for much in the liturgical scheme of things, we were nevertheless, in such a small church, painfully exposed to the general gaze. I remembered my grandfather, back home in North Shields, safe in his organ loft, above the fray, keeping his dignity.

For all my desperate pedalling, and despite pulling out all the stops, the harmonium was never more than a half-hearted partner. Its voice squeaked pitiably, a gnat's whistle, not even a cheap parody of its chapel betters. Fortunately, our congregation was correspondingly thin. Indeed, there seemed to be a tacit acknowledgement that we were well suited, singers, instrument and instrumentalist alike. None would outshine the others. 'So much nicer than before,' they said, politely.

I would normally be called into action only on Sundays and the main feast days. Our repertory was not, however, limited to hymns. After two years of desultory progress, and despite our many deficiencies, we mustered enough confidence to have a go at singing the mass itself. It was all in unison, of course, and we used a score that did not make excessive demands either in the upper or lower registers. Indeed, only by the skin of its teeth could it be called music at all. But it was a step in the right direction. It wasn't chapel, but it was distinctively ours. At last, we were holding our end up.

As was common in Catholic parishes, the faithful went to confession either immediately before mass or else on the previous day. On the occasion in question I chose to go on the Saturday, trusting that it would be less busy, that I would have more time for the important confession I needed to make. I didn't know exactly how long it would take—how could I?—but I doubted whether I'd be off my knees in less than ten minutes, and I didn't want to be rushed. And then there was the penance. That was certain to be more than the usual Hail Mary, Our Father and Glory Be, and I had to have it all done and dusted before taking up my position at the organ. No penance, no absolution: that was the rule. Absolution was a prized commodity in those days and you had to pay the full price. God wasn't one for the never-never.

But there was another reason I chose Saturday over Sunday. On Sunday I should have to make my confession and then endure the additional humiliation of returning to the body of the church to face my fellow penitents. They would be few, it is true, but each had two eyes and a watch and enough acquaintance with sin to conclude that my confession consisted of more than the usual litany of curses and fibs and over-indulgence. They'd already have seen Veronica Doyle go up, like she did every week, face shrouded in her mantilla and everyone knowing why. Hadn't we seen her dancing with Stephen Murray in the Union the night before? Didn't we remember his hands, all over her? And then me. I'd go after her, delay proceedings for another ten minutes, and everybody would say, Aye, aye, there's another one. Wonder who with?

I didn't have such thick skin. Such bottle.

On Saturdays you didn't go to the church, you went to the presbytery. This, I presume, was for the convenience of the priest, who could not be expected to sit idly in his gloomy little box on the off-chance that someone would call by. The presbytery abutted on to the church. It had neither name nor number, but the whole ensemble, on a little rise opposite the police station, was known as Mount Carmel. Painted in white, with pastel-shaded shutters at the windows and fronted by a large, all-weather crucifix, it was an act of faith in the apostolic mission in these parts. I knocked on the front door a little before four o'clock in the afternoon. Father O'Casey himself answered.

'Just happened to be passing,' I said, in as casual a manner as I could. Then explained my purpose.

'Mm,' he said. He seemed to be chewing something. Then, 'It will be easier to talk upstairs.' And wiped his lips. There were crumbs on his cardigan.

'I'm sorry to disturb your ...' I stopped there, unsure whether it was his dinner or his tea he'd been eating.

We went up to Father O'Casey's bedroom. This was the routine on Mount Carmel. The confessional was used only on Sundays, when time was of the essence, and the stream of penitents had to be kept moving so that mass could begin promptly. It should also be remembered that Father O'Casey was a genial and unassuming man who enjoyed the company of like-minded souls. Alas, such company was a scarce commodity in these parts: his flock was sparse and scattered, and he the sole shepherd. He was glad of whatever human intercourse came his way, even if it was of the penitential kind. Nor was there anything untoward in the use of his bedroom as a surrogate confessional. The incumbent of Mount Carmel had, in fact, only one room to call his own: the others were let to students, to eke out his meagre allowance. It was in this room that Father O'Casey lived the greater part of his life.

I could smell bacon. So, it was his dinner. A late dinner. Or else an early tea, of course. Bacon and, I think, fried bread. Then I saw the plate on the table by the window. The knife and fork.

'Where should I ...?'

There was no need to kneel, he said. So I perched on the corner of Father O'Casey's bed, while he drew up a wooden chair and sat facing me. He took his stole in both hands, drew it up to his lips and gave it a silent kiss. Then he placed it around his neck and bowed his head in prayer. I bowed my own head. I was now close enough to see the patches of eczema on his brow, the little flakes of peeling skin. And I couldn't tell whether it was the room or else Father O'Casey himself that smelled of bacon. Both, more than likely.

It would, in any case, have been difficult to kneel down in this room. There was neither kneeler nor hassock. More significantly, the whole floor—with the exception of a narrow pathway between the door and the bed— was occupied by empty bottles, some standing, the majority lying on their sides. I saw mainly vodka bottles. The simple elegance of the Wodka Wyborowa label was easy to recognise. (Presents from the many Poles in the parish, I presumed.) But there were also at least two bottles of Hirondelle. None was full; in fact, none that I could see contained a single drop. I did my best to avert my gaze. Father O'Casey seemed oblivious to it all, perhaps through force of habit. I wondered where the unopened bottles were kept. There must have been a cupboard somewhere, more than likely in the little kitchen on the other side of the landing. My heels discovered more bottles under the bed. We both ignored the little *chink*.

'Bless me, Father, for I have sinned ...'

I made my confession. I started with Wednesday's spate of indulgence, when I ate seven chocolate puddings in the college refectory. Not that I counted this a particularly weighty sin: the puddings belonged to my fellow students and a much greater sin, to my mind, was to take them in the first place and then fail to consume them. But I needed something inconsequential of the sort to prepare the way. Then I told him how I'd been a little abrupt (I said 'uncharitable') with the woman in the bread shop when she'd short-changed me. (By fifty pence, I should add.) And

I rummaged about for something else then, to buy a little more time, because by then I was beginning to yearn for the anonymity of the confessional, the dark wood, the dividing screen, its little grill sufficient, you might suppose, to render one person's guilty whispers much like another's.

Then, having exhausted the venial sins, I moved on to the main item. I followed the euphemistic formula. I received the time-honoured response.

'With yourself or with others?'

I had prepared my script.

'With one other.'

Pause. I believe Father O'Casey was suffering from wind. He tightened his lips, waited for the spasm to pass.

'A girl?'

'Yes. We love each other. We intend getting engaged soon.'

Father O'Casey rearranged his feet. 'You mean ...' He cleared his throat. 'You're saying that the two of you had sexual intercourse, yes?'

'Yes.' And said this a little too eagerly, glad to have it out at last. I answered again, with more reserve. 'Yes, we did.'

Another pause. My confessor's indigestion was clearly causing him discomfort. He swallowed hard.

'How many times?'

'Once ...' Again, too forcibly. And not quite right, either. 'No, twice. But on the same day. Twice on the same day. One after the ...' I felt my cheeks burn.

Father O'Casey rearranged his feet again. He straightened up and struck his chest with his right fist, just as though he were saying a swift *mea culpa*. But this was the bacon talking. He hiccupped, beat his chest again.

'You know that God ...' Then hiccupped again. 'You know that God reserved the act of love for those who have joined themselves together in marriage ...'

I nodded. 'Yes, Father,' I said, happy to agree, trying to sound contrite.

'And that it is a sin—a grievous sin, a mortal sin—to engage in sexual intercourse outside of marriage?'

I nodded again.

'And each occasion, too. Each commission of the act is a denial of our Heavenly Father's plan for us. No matter with whom, nor when. You understand?'

'Yes.'

He bowed his head, looked at the floor. I could see now that the eczema had spread to his eyebrows and that the hairs had little feathers of dry skin between them. I wondered, if I drew a finger through those hairs, whether the feathers would lose their grip and float down, like a little flurry of snow, onto the bottles.

'... a sin especially against the Holy Family ...'

'Yes, Father.'

'... a sin that causes great suffering to God's own Mother, a sin against her unblemished virtue ...'

'Yes, Father.'

'And are you truly sorry for this sin?'

'Yes, I am, Father.'

'And do you truly and utterly repent and reject that sin and promise to make a firm resolution not to put yourself again in the way of temptation?

'I do, Father.'

'Good. Now make a sincere act of contrition.'

For my penance, Father O'Casey told me to say the whole rosary. Although this would take a great deal more than ten minutes, I was relieved. I had imagined some more arduous and unusual reparation for such grievous wrongdoing. He also told me to meditate on the Holy Family and the Virgin Mother and her unblemished virtue and the great offence I had caused her and to make a picture of her in my mind every time I thought I might succumb. This, too, presented no new challenges. I could close my eyes and conjure up the blue and white Our Lady of Grace statue that stood in the church, just to the left of the harmonium. True, it was not the Virgin Mother herself, but I was confident that the heavy folded robes, the pale expressionless face, the plaster frigidity of it all, were close enough to what Father O'Casey had in mind. Then he gave me absolution. 'In the name of the Farther, and the Son and the Holy Ghost ....' He removed his stole and hung it over the back of the chair.

Before I left he looked through the window. 'Rain on the way,' he said. Then, as though he were still talking about the weather: 'There's nothing the church can do, you know.'

'No,' I said. I was keen to leave and get my penance done, but I knew there was more to come, that the confession and the penance weren't the half of it. Father O'Casey continued to stand at the window, studying the clouds, hiccupping quietly.

'If she weren't still married, of course ... I mean, in the eyes of the church ...' He looked over at me, to see whether I was catching his drift. 'If she hadn't ... I mean, if she could show the marriage hadn't been ...'

He paused. I thought. Or, rather, I tried to contrive thoughts where there were none to be had. I wanted to say, 'But how could she? I mean, what would she ...?' I said nothing. I shrugged.

Father O'Casey shook his head, looked at the floor, lips tight in resignation. Hiccupped. 'No, I suppose not.'

I opened the door. 'Thanks for ...'

'Of course you don't have to ... What I mean is, you're always welcome to ...' He looked through the window again, searched for the words, looked back at me. 'Everyone is very appreciative of what you've done here ... what you still do ... playing the organ and so on ... 'I nodded, mustered a faint smile. 'What I mean to say is, you'd be very welcome to come back. At any time. To play the organ, that is. I mean, if things should ... with Delyth ... you understand ...? In fact, if you want to continue as before ... I mean, every Sunday ... there's no need to, you know ... just because ...'

100

For a moment I savoured this brief reversal, Father O'Casey's reincarnation as supplicant. I offered a ruminative 'Mm.' Then I said, 'I'm not sure. I'll have to think about that.'

I didn't return to Mount Carmel to play the harmonium. Nor did I meditate on the plaster virgin. I lost faith in the God of the confessional and the empty bottles. I wasn't tempted to embrace any other god, either, at least not for the time being. I did, however, heed the teachings of the chapel on the edge of town: that nothing was predestined, that our will was free and our own, and that reason should be its guide. Following that guide, I began to attend services. I sat with Delyth in her customary pew while her mother, twin-setted and pudding-hatted, delivered her rich harmonies from above. I contributed a hesitant, muted bass. I did not go often, but I went as often as reason required, until all could see that I'd submitted to her sway. Six months later, somewhat against the grain, she played for our wedding. The trumpets of Zion rang out.

A Visit from the Police

It's mid-day, sometime between Christmas and New Year. I'm sitting in our local with David, my brother, his wife, Stefanie, and Mam. David's drinking a pint of Vaux. Mam and Stefanie have small medium sherries. I've chosen ginger beer: drinking alcohol at lunchtime makes me drowsy for the rest of the day. Stefanie's reciting the menu, line by line, because Mam can't read the small print. This lunch is a treat for Mam, to say thanks for having us over the Christmas. The Alexandra is a modern, soulless place, and the food isn't much to boast about either. But it's convenient. And since we've had to leave Dad at home by himself we daren't venture any further. That's what Mam said. 'We'll go to the Alexandra.' Meaning, if we've got to go anywhere, that's where we'll go. So that we can be on hand. So that she won't have to fret. And even then, only for an hour and a half. Ninety minutes. And ten of them have already been used up, walking the fifty yards from the house, taking off our coats, ordering the drinks.

For myself, I don't need to study the menu in detail. There is only one vegetarian option: the mushroom stroganov. David and Stefanie dither, quite unnecessarily, shaking their heads at the paucity of choice. 'Come on, David,' says Mam. The food is of no importance to her: all she's concerned about today is getting back home by half past one.

Knowing that he has only an hour and a half—because that's what Mam told him, when we left: 'Back by half past one'—Dad has surely already begun to stir: when he heard the door close, perhaps, and the *clunk* of the gate afterwards. He knows exactly what needs to be done, because surely he has been rehearsing every step in his mind throughout the night and morning. He's been calculating, should I go this way or that? Would it be quicker if I did such-and-such? And I shouldn't be surprised if he's dreamed about it as well, about this little unexpected journey. What kind of dreams were they? Were they full of anticipation and excitement? Or were they haunted by fear and anxiety? A mixture, no doubt.

But no, Dad won't have made his move quite so soon. So perhaps not when the door closed. Or even the gate. Dad would surely wait a little, just to make sure that Mam didn't come back, as she often does, fearing that she's left the oven on, or the upstairs light, or hasn't locked the side door. He'd hold his horses, just to be on the safe side. But not too much, either. Although Dad has planned each step quite meticulously, as meticulously as a general mapping out his plan of attack, he knows quite well that it will be touch and go, because there's no telling what the enemy will do next.

Five minutes. Let's say that Dad delays for five minutes. He tells himself, 'Right, they'll not come back now. I can make my move.' But move what? His hand? Yes, I should think so. It's the hand that must move first. To take hold of the sheets, the blankets. The right hand, too, so that he can pull them the correct way, towards the window. Because the other side, the left side, is the side he must get out of bed. And there's nothing the matter with his arms. Even after five years in bed, his arms still work like well-oiled pistons. He can change channels on the television with his stick. He can throw a plate of stew and mashed potato at the wall when he loses his temper. So I'm sure he has no difficulty pulling off the bedclothes, at least enough to free his legs. He'll have to bend forward a little, of course, and I've no doubt that it hurts his back to do so. That's his weak spot, the back, where the growth is. But he gets by. Somehow, he manages. There's no time to be lost, and it's amazing what a man can do, what a man is ready to endure, when his minutes are numbered.

This is when Dad's labours start in earnest. For it is here, on the left side of his bed, that the urine bag is attached. I say 'attached' because I assume that the bag must be tied, somehow, to the frame of the bed. I am guessing somewhat, as I have not actually seen the straps and buckles, but this is what seems reasonable. The bag has been tied securely to the bed in such a way as to minimise movement of the connecting tube, so that the bag, as it fills, as it becomes heavier, is prevented from pulling on the catheter.

Having drawn the bedclothes over far enough to give himself freedom of movement, Dad turns onto his left side, so he can get at the knots, the straps, the buckles, whatever is there. He reaches out both hands, because a man needs all his fingers and thumbs to undo a knot, to unfasten a buckle. This is surely quite a tricky manoeuvre: his left arm must still be under his body, and I'm not sure, on reflection, whether he has the strength to raise himself on his elbow. But, somehow or other, this is what he does, what he must do. There is no other way to effect an escape from the bed except through unfastening the straps, detaching the bag and the tube. He pokes his head over the edge, to get a better view of things.

Dad's plan is nothing if not ambitious. He hasn't got out of bed by himself for several years. I can only admire such single-minded determination. Determination, and a degree of dexterity, too: he'll need more than his customary bloody-mindedness to get to grips with this little conundrum, and no mistake. Do the muscles remember, I wonder? And the nerves? Do they still recognise knots and buckles? And even if they do remember, can they then be roused from their long idleness and persuaded to do just one more stint of work? Yes, he's got the will, but has he got the means?

I don't know the answers to these questions: I can merely guess, try to put two and two together. But this is how it must be, surely. This is what common sense tells me has to be the case. And as I say, I can only admire such dogged dedication.

When I go to fetch a second pint for my brother and a sherry each for Mam and Stefanie, Dad's feet are already on the floor. I've no idea how he's done this but it's an indisputable fact because, without first getting his feet on the floor, how can he progress further? His feet are on the floor and he's holding on to the sheets as tightly as he can: he doesn't want to fall and I doubt whether he has enough strength in his legs to bear his weight any more. So, feet on the floor, arse sticking up in the air, fingers gripping tight, face red with the strain, knuckles white. That's how it is, for a few seconds. But such tension cannot be sustained for long. And when he does let go, when the fingers loosen their grip on the sheets, his knees drop to the floor with a sudden thud that shakes his whole body, even rattles his teeth. (Does he have his teeth in?) He has to pause, to get his breath back, his composure, to make sure no damage has been done. He leans his forearms on the bed, and perhaps his head, too. A little break, to gather his strength for the next stage. He looks at the bag and the catheter, checks that nothing's come loose during his little tumble. That's what Dad does.

'He'll come round,' says Mam.

My brother shrugs his shoulders and pulls a face, as if to say, 'What does it matter?'

'We weren't making any noise,' says Stefanie.

'No, I know you weren't,' says Mam.

'Just wanted to stay down a bit longer.'

'Yes.'

'Go to bed in our own time.'

'Yes, I know.'

'We weren't noisy.'

And it's true. I didn't hear any noise at all. Nothing, except Dad, banging the floor with his stick.

The biggest feat, then, is to get hold of the bag—and the tube as well, of course, and goodness knows how many straps and buckles—to take hold of these things with his left hand and transfer his weight to the right. In doing so, he must hold the tube with the greatest delicacy, taking care not to pull it too tight but at the same time ensuring that it doesn't drag on the floor and get caught by his knee. For what, then, would happen to the catheter? No, he doesn't want his catheter to come out. Whatever else happens to Dad today, he needs his catheter to stay put. If it came out he would have to put it back in, and I've heard the screams myself. That's how I know he won't risk it, not for anything. So he holds the tube as delicately, as attentively, as though he were holding his own heart.

The worst is now over. That, at least, is how it appears to me. If my Dad can coordinate hand and eye, arm and leg, finger and thumb, sufficiently well to get this far, to get his feet on the floor and his hands and knees as well, then what is left but to keep on going? He crawls to the door. The door is always ajar, so he doesn't have to reach for the handle. He need only pull it towards himself a little and out he goes.

He's at the top of the stairs.

Now then, I've no doubt it would be easier, had Dad fuller mastery over his limbs, were his spine more supple, for him to descend on his backside. Leading with his feet and supporting his weight on his right hand, he could then lower himself down, step by step, like a little child. Perhaps that is, indeed, what he has decided to do. To give it a go, anyway. I can only hazard a guess. I'm sure I shall never know, because who would presume to ask? Who would dare? 'Dad, did you come down the stairs on your arse?' Who would be so stupid?

Yes, all this is possible. What is more likely, however, is that Dad decides to come downstairs on all fours. Having weighed up the various options, having estimated the time each would take, having made vivid images in his mind of the perils and pitfalls, he has decided to crawl. Crawling is by now second nature to him, and although crawling backwards downstairs is quite a challenge to one who has ventured no further than the bathroom in five years, the basic movements, the essential techniques are the same. Crawling is crawling. Even if a leg slipped, even if he had a dizzy spell, which happens from time to time, this would be no particular cause for concern: he could simply lay his arms on the step in front of him, and his head too if he wished, and take a swift breather. None of this would be possible if he descended on his backside. One slip, one nasty turn, and that would be the end of him: the tube would slip from his grasp, he'd reach out for it, but in his haste, in his desperation, he would reach too far, and there he'd be, a second later, tumbling head over heels to the bottom of the stairs. And dear knows what state he'd be in then. So that's how it is. A climber must always face the rock, even when descending. Dad is a climber. He knows he must obey the rules.

At the top of the stairs Dad pauses briefly to collect his thoughts. In the pub, Mam is already looking at her watch, is starting to feel anxious, even though it is only one o'clock and she hasn't eaten half her dinner. 'Not used to it, you see.' That's her excuse. 'Not this time of day.' Pudding? No, thank you. Coffee? No, thank you. Never drinks coffee in the afternoon. Another sherry? Perhaps when she gets home. She rummages in her purse and I have to remind her that this is her treat today, that we are paying. 'To say thank you,' says Stefanie. She knows this, of course, but this is her way of declaring to everyone that she is ready to leave. My brother's at the bar, ordering another pint. He's in no hurry to go anywhere.

'You must come!'

Stefanie tells us about the decorating they've been doing in their house in Guildford and tries to persuade Mam to come and stay for a few days at Easter, or perhaps in the summer, when the weather's better. She suggests putting Dad into a rest home, just for a few days, a week at the most. She talks about the places they might visit, the shops, the friends. But no-one says anything more about last night, or about going back to the house. The purpose of this occasion is to pretend for a while that, despite a few surface ripples, the waters beneath remain calm and unthreatening. Everything will turn out for the best. Mam recognises this pretence, too, or she would not have come out in the first place. It is a strain. But normality will soon return. Tomorrow she will be by herself again.

Dad has no watch but he can feel his heart beating faster, and that is quite as good as a ticking clock, telling him to get a move on. He knows, from long acquaintance, that Mam will be fidgeting by now, that she will already be seeking some way of returning home early, that he has perhaps no more than half an hour to complete his task. So get a move on. Put your foot down. That's what he's saying to himself. The last thing he wants is to be stranded down there, at the foot of the stairs, piss bag in hand, when we come in through the front door. To be caught in the act. So, half an hour. And Dad's wondering, will that be enough?

That's why he starts working out a little schedule, to put his mind at rest. He asks himself: How many steps are there, then? Sixteen? Eighteen? Twenty at the most. Right, then. How much time do I need for each step? That sort of thing. But his patience runs out and he gives up. In any case, he's already made up his mind. He knows this is a time for action, not fine calculation. And what, he thinks, is there to worry about? One step at a time, and each step the same, no surprises there, and carry on until he reaches the bottom. And he'll no doubt pick up a bit of speed, too, as he gets the hang of it. A little stop now and again, just a few seconds, to rest his arm. He can feel it already, the weight of the urine bag, the strain in his elbow and forearm. So, just two or three stops, then on with the show. Yes, half an hour will be quite enough.

David puts his pint on the table and picks up the menu. 'You're not having pudding, are you?' says Stefanie, who is also starting to feel uneasy. Mam's anxiety is contagious. My brother says 'Yes', with a studied nonchalance. But he's talking to Dad, really, not to Stefanie. He's telling Dad that the family is staking its claim to this little interlude of autonomy and is not to be budged, come what may. 'It's alright for you,' Mam says. 'You're going home tomorrow.' And everybody goes quiet for a minute.

Stefanie asks me about the children. She does this, I think, because I haven't said much so far and also, perhaps, because I seem not to have been tainted either by Mam's nerves or by my brother's stubbornness. She asks about my work, too, and about holidays, and we meander from topic to topic for a few minutes, trying to make the best of it, my brother throwing in the odd waggish comment to give the impression that this is really where he wants to be, chatting amiably with his family, drinking his pint, savouring each mouthful of his Black Forest Gateau.

One step at a time, and each step the same, and carry on until he reaches the bottom. Easier said than done. And that's where my guessing game comes unstuck, of course, because how can I possibly divine the inner workings of another's body? The arm, held in the air, carrying the bag and the tube, is under strain. But everything else is under strain, too. The spine, for example, abruptly deprived of mattress and pillow, that must now bear the whole body's weight. The muscles, tendons and sinews in his legs, which he does his best to rally to the cause, but to little effect, so that the knees strike harder with each step. *Bump, bump.* And his body now swaying from side to side as he does do, because he has only one hand free to keep his balance, to hold on to the stairs. But he daren't sway too much, or what will happen to the catheter? And under such strain, each step demanding greater effort than the one before, until there comes a point—at the turn in the stairs, perhaps— when the next step is harder even than getting out of bed, because the bed was just one thing, and the first thing at that.

But somehow, bruised, breathless and exhausted, he reaches the bottom of the stairs. This is where the telephone is located. It's just as well, too: I doubt whether he could have made it much further. The telephone stands on a small shelf of his own making, and at a height, as it happens, that is quite convenient for one who must proceed on all fours. The directory is at hand, too, and he will need to refer to this, I'm sure, to get the number. I'm guessing again, but it is scarcely credible that the number hasn't changed in twenty years. So that's what he does. He looks for the new number. Which means that he must have brought his specs with him. Where did he put his specs while he descended the stairs? Well, in the pocket of his pyjama jacket, most likely. And that's another good reason for coming downstairs arse first: the specs are less at risk of falling out of the pocket. And if they did so, they would not fall far.

He writes the number on the pad. Yes, there is a pad there, too, and a pencil. He writes down the number, in big bold figures because, when he's dialling, that will be easier to read than the number in the directory. In any case, it would be difficult to do both things at once: to dial and also to keep the directory open and in view. The shelf is, I think, too small for such acrobatics. If he sat down, of course, he could rest the book in his lap. But that is not possible. He is crawling. He is on all fours. And in any case, this is how he's already planned it all. The pencil. The pad.

Dad dials the number. It rings. A voice answers. I'm not sure whether he asks for anyone in particular. Is there still someone there, I wonder, some Sergeant, some Inspector, who was a constable in the old days and might remember him? Not merely remember, either, but, in some small way, cherish that memory. Or at least be well enough disposed that Dad feels entitled to ask him a favour. No, I think not. Not after so many years. And even if there is, I doubt whether he's in the mood for reminiscence. He might lose the thread and waste valuable time gathering it in again. No beating about the bush, then. He must get straight to the point. And this, after all, is his way of doing things. The police way.

'I've got two people here trespassing on my property. I want you to come and move them on.'

Yes, this is his way. But Dad realises that he's raced ahead of himself a little. In his eagerness to get the words out, to convey the meat of the message, he has neglected the proper sequence of events. Which is no surprise, of course. What else would one expect, after twenty years? And bearing in mind his temperament, his impatience to get matters settled.

'Your name and address, sir?'

After giving his details, Dad pauses a second, half expecting some flicker of recognition. 'Did you say Bianchi? Is that the George Bianchi that used to be here?' Something like that. But the young man at the end of the line just moves on to the next question. 'And who are these people, sir, who refuse to leave your property?'

I am sure this question has been simmering in Dad's mind for some hours. Not the question itself, but its implications. One so thorough in his preparations, so familiar with the relevant procedures for the gathering and recording of information, will have considered this matter

111

from every possible angle. And that is why he is able to answer swiftly and decisively.

'My son and his wife. I need you to come at once and remove them from my premises. They are trespassing.'

Dad knows it is not so much the content of his message that counts but rather the manner of its delivery. He needs to show that he is in earnest, that he is a seasoned operator where the law is concerned, that he wishes to deal with this matter firmly and dispassionately. And that trespass is trespass, no matter what the pedigree of the offender.

'Your son, sir?'

'Yes, and his wife. They are trespassing. They refuse to leave my property. I need you to come at once. As a matter of urgency.'

This is what he says. This is what he has rehearsed throughout the night and morning. He gets it right first time. And yet, no sooner have the words left his lips than he begins to regret being quite so adamant. Perhaps, he thinks, the police, in responding to his quite persuasive urgency, will indeed come at once, a full half hour before our return from the pub. And he doesn't want that. He doesn't want the police to arrive and find no trespassers on the property. 'They'll be back now, officer. They've just slipped out for a bite to eat.' That wouldn't do at all. Nor does he want the police to see him crawling on the floor like an old tortoise, to see him holding his piss bag in the air.

Perhaps, by now, he even regrets the whole episode as he turns around and looks at the stairs and thinks, 'Jesus, how am I going to get back up them?'

By the time we return, he's back in bed. I'm not sure how long he's been there but when Mam goes up to say that we're home, he's fast asleep. We have a cup of tea then and relax in front of the kitchen fire. We are all relieved to be home. We regret going out in the first place. But nothing is said.

The policeman calls by half an hour later to tell us about the phone call, to make sure that everything's alright. He has a cup of tea, too, and chats with Mam about the old days, when Dad was in the force, when they went on the beat two at a time, when the criminals were more colourful. She tells him about the villains she's met down the years. 'Met a murderer in the Jungle once,' she says. 'Town's altered a lot since then, mind.' With a pretence of nostalgia in her voice.

The policeman tells her to ring him if she has problems. 'Any time,' he says. 'Always glad to be of help.' We're pleased to hear this. And it's a comfort to Mam, because she'll be by herself again tomorrow.

The Bench

As an outsider, I loved Cardiff's parks because I so little expected them. Cardiff, in my mind's caricature, was no more than a giant coal chute, a conduit for getting Wales's black gold out to the world. It was a point of passage, of exchange; a grey, one-dimensional sort of place.

Reality, as always, was more variegated and contradictory. The Scottish Marquis of Bute financed the Welsh Coalopolis, and it was he, too, who conjured a rustic refuge at its heart. Standing here, by the Gothic extravaganza of Cardiff Castle, I see nothing but fields, trees and, in the distance, the fairy towers of Bute's other act of grand whimsy, Castell Coch. It is all a masterpiece of picturesque illusion.

I am free to yield to this illusion, to immerse myself in it, because Bute's private retreat is now Bute Park, a vast public garden extending from the city centre to the edge of Llandaff. Here, and particularly in the famous *arboretum*, with its exotic trees and flowers, I can find instant respite from the city's bustle. Here, the city 'wraps around me', as the poet Emyr Lewis says, but with gentle arms. Cardiff is small enough to be both city and sanctuary; intimate enough to make you feel at home, even if you are not a native.

Most enter Bute Park through its South Gate, near the Animal Wall. This high divide between city and park is guarded by vivid stone sculptures of bear, lynx, vulture and other very un-Welsh creatures, as though to remind us that we are entering a place of strangeness. From here, a path winds between Cowper's Field and the Castle Grounds. It is this path which I myself followed most weekdays for twenty years, making my way to the office in the morning and returning home at evening. Frequently, whenever work and weather permitted, I would return here at lunchtime, to eat my sandwiches, to read the papers, and perhaps have a nap.

Following this routine, I came to know the lower reaches of the park quite intimately. I learned the order in which the trees came into leaf: the *acer* in March, for example, the *paulownia* at the end of April, and last of all, without fail, the Japanese *katsura*, with its beautiful heart-shaped leaves. I looked forward eagerly to their transformation, in autumn, from lush green to fantastic shades of yellow, purple and red. I relished the powerful and improbable aroma of burnt sugar. I rejoiced at the flowering of cherry and magnolia and grieved as November winds stripped all bare.

My usual sitting place, on these visits, was a green wooden bench. This stood on the north side of the path and looked out over the Gorsedd stone circle (another Victorian fabrication) towards the castle's ornate clock tower. And although the park was a popular destination on a warm summer afternoon, I generally had this bench to myself. Why, I'm not sure: I think that others preferred to be by the river, or else under the trees, sitting on the grass. The bench was, for them, perhaps not sufficiently in one place or another. Whatever the case, it is true that I came to feel, in the end, that I had something of a claim upon it, a claim that other pedestrians had learned to respect. I certainly felt put out if, on crossing the small bridge over the feeder, I saw that it was occupied by someone else. If the bench was in truth a rather plain and uncomfortable piece of furniture, it had nevertheless become a kind of pivot for my daily round, the calm centre to which I returned for some security and solace. I have always been a creature of habit.

Although, as I say, this path between the two fields was a popular thoroughfare and a convenient meeting place for many, I generally came alone. Sufficient for me my thoughts and the beautiful surroundings. And yet my sojourns here, on the green bench, were not entirely devoid of human company. After all, I was hardly the only citizen whose daily life followed a predictable pattern. It was only natural, therefore, as the months and years passed, that I came to recognise and greet many who walked this way. With some, I conversed. Take the poet, R. S. Thomas, for example. No, not the Rev. R. S. Thomas, but Bob S. Thomas, from Llanelli: a claw-fingered, ragged-haired rhymester somewhat less elevated than that great harrier of the Welsh conscience. Bob would rest here a while, to have a chat, to rail at the world, to smoke a cigarette, before resuming his journey along the river path.

Some encounters were, naturally, more memorable than others. In 1980, I enjoyed a few precious moments here in the company of Derek Walcott, as I accompanied him to his hotel. (Walcott received our International Writer's Prize that year.) He was much amused by the stone circle and the castle, although I believe he thought them somewhat absurd. He was, of course, too courteous to say as much: they are, after all, part of our national iconography. He was also delighted to learn that Joseph Conrad had once lived nearby: Conrad had been his teacher's favourite author at school in Saint Lucia. Somehow, I believe Walcott saw all of these things—the stones, the castle, Conrad's residence here—as part of some single pattern. This is perhaps the privilege of the visitor, who sees our familiar world through fresh eyes.

Unfortunately, not every visitor was as gracious as the Caribbean poet. Two years later I sat on the same bench, this time in the company of my two young children, when I received a ferocious kick to my right shin from none other than the daughter of Margaret Atwood. (It was the Canadian novelist's turn to receive our prize in that year.) Jessica was her name, I think: a spirited six year old who had become tired of touring the world. I suspect I was a convenient whipping-boy and I took my punishment like a dutiful public servant. I'm sure I recall this trivial incident, however, not because of the pain I endured but because of the location. The bench—my *locus standi*, I think you would call it—has pinned the event to my memory like an insect to a mount.

1982 was the year of the kick. This, too, was the year of the strangest of all my encounters, although it did not strike me as such at the time. It was a Saturday afternoon in April. As it happens, I wasn't sitting on the bench, owing to a sharp wind; instead, I stood to one side, doing stretching exercises, keeping warm, in preparation for a game of football. This is what had been arranged for that unseasonally cold afternoon: a kick-about between work colleagues and some of my neighbours from Riverside. I had been given a black and white striped Newcastle United shirt for my birthday and I wore it with that boyish pride in which Tynesiders habitually indulge when away from home.

And perhaps it is the shirt that was to blame.

He asked me for a light: a strange thing to do, you might think, given that I was so clearly preparing myself for physical exercise, but there it is—I was the only person to hand. He was a young man, dressed in the casual clothes of the day: jeans, trainers, leather jacket, black woollen hat. His face was, in retrospect, quite distinctive: his nose long and thin, but broadening somewhat where it joined the forehead. But I'm not sure whether this struck me at the time. If I'd had to guess at his origins, I would have suggested Italy, or perhaps Greece. He said little. In fact, at this stage, he did not actually speak, but rather mimed the action of lighting a match and pointed at the cigarette in his mouth. Only after the first inhalation, after proffering a smile of thanks, did the words come. And they came reluctantly, hesitantly, each heavily accented.

'You ... your ... team?' he said, eying my shirt.

I nodded.

'Me ... my team,' he said. 'My team ... mm ... Like this ... but red and white.'

'Ah,' I replied, facetiously. 'Sunderland.'

I am sure he understood nothing of football rivalries in the north-east of England. In any case, he had no opportunity to respond. At that moment, I heard a shout behind me and there they were, my friends, my colleagues, arriving for our game of football. I judged that the polite course of action would be to ask my new acquaintance if he wished to join in. And this he did. He took off his jacket and hat and played in our game for half an hour or so. I cannot say now whether he performed well or not, although it would have been no great feat to excel amongst rank amateurs such as ourselves. When

he left he smiled, raised his hand and said, quietly, 'Thank you, thank you.' This is what I remember.

Eighteen years passed before I saw that face again. Scenes from a funeral were being broadcast on BBC News 24. Soldiers in formation, firing in the air. Women grieving. A coffin being lowered into the ground. And then, a picture of him, the laconic footballer. Young, but not as he was; rather, as he had become, after that day in the park. And, for me, so incongruous in his combat gear. Because this was the face of Zeliko Raznotivic or, to give him his more familiar name, Arkan. And if you remember Vukovar, if you remember the hundreds dragged from their hospital beds, driven to a remote field and shot in the head, then you will remember Arkan. That was his war. And in the armies of that war's damned, Arkan outranked them all.

I asked myself afterwards what Arkan might have been doing in Cardiff, of all places, on that unremarkable day. I tried my best to piece together the facts and make from them a credible story. Arkan was a fugitive in 1982, of that I could be certain. He had escaped from a prison in Frankfurt (he had escaped from several other prisons on previous occasions) and was still at large. Was that an adequate reason? That he had to be somewhere? That Cardiff was a suitable refuge, precisely because it was such an unremarkable place? Then, somehow, without further legal intervention, he returned to Belgrade and opened a *patisserie*. Who would believe it? But that was his trade. And this is a fact, too: irrefutable, confirmed by all the websites. It appears that it was a popular *patisserie*. Its cakes were of the highest quality. And then the killing. When everything fell apart. There's no doubting that, either. Only one mystery remained: the gap. Cardiff and the bench in the park and the game of football and us. (I say us. There may be others, there must be others, but how can I speak for them?) We were the mystery.

I began to doubt myself. I became frustrated with my inability to put them side-by-side, the picture in the memory and the picture on the screen. I wanted to go up to the judge and declare, confidently, authoritatively, 'Look at this, sir. Do you see the long fine nose? Do you see how it broadens somewhat where it meets the brow? The eyes, too. And the mouth. Look, they are the same.' But the memory is incapable of producing such pictures. And what other proof could I offer? What other evidence do I have that this, indeed, was the man in the park, and not some other, anonymous stranger? To the unfamiliar eye, to the untutored ear—please forgive me for saying this, I'm simply trying to be honest— are not all strangers somewhat alike? Perhaps not all, no, of course not all, but many. And I know we are reluctant to acknowledge the fact. Indeed, such clichés make us feel uncomfortable, unenlightened, unclean. But I believe there is a grain of truth in what I am saying.

And that, perhaps, is how I would have consoled myself, by wrapping my defective memory in the cotton wool of cliché. Yes, it must have been someone else. Someone from the same part of the world, no doubt. From the Balkans. Otherwise it would be such a coincidence, it would be so melodramatic. And who would believe me? You're pulling our legs, they'd say, if I told them, if I got in touch with my colleagues and friends, if I could track them down. That's not him, they'd say. Can't be. Just looks a bit like him. Like they do, over there. And how could I prove otherwise?

And that might well have been true. Except for the shirt. If he hadn't mentioned the shirt. The shirt was the final proof, the fact that cannot be ignored. Or, rather, the two shirts: the red and white, of course, which he gladly, even boastfully acknowledged; but also the black and white. Without the black and white, surely the red and white would never have been mentioned. No, not the shirts of Newcastle and Sunderland—this was a fanciful, childish notion from some far, forgotten land—but those of Crvena Zvezda and Partizan. Both, in equal measure. Arkan's Tigers.

Departure

It starts well enough. The flight is on time. We get through security without mishap. On board, we strap ourselves in and yield to the ritual of the pre-flight safety demonstration: confirmation that ordinary life has been put into abeyance. The two attendants clip and unclip their seatbelts, don their life jackets and oxygen masks, indicate the emergency exits, all with synchronised smiles and such fluid choreography that part of you thinks perhaps the coming disaster will be quite a benign business after all, or at least impeccably tasteful.

The take-off disrupts our camaraderie. I say, 'Seems calm enough today.' Clare closes her eyes, clenches her fists. We all become tight-lipped during the brief but desperate tug-of-war between the aircraft and the runway's clinging asphalt; at the judders, creaks and whinnies; at the sheer improbability of it all. But then we rise through the clouds and emerge into the bright blue skyscape. Up here we are weightless, detached, tugged along gently by the sun's golden cord. The earth, once dark and heavy, has become just a smudge between clouds. Gravity has been vanquished. The wings' confident arrow tells us we know where we are going.

'Italy,' she said. 'Italy would be nice.'

'The lakes?' I suggested.

It seemed the right thing to say at the time. Lying there, after sex, which was still tentative, too much calculation, not enough letting go. I hadn't realised letting go would be so hard to learn. Then looking out through the window, at the thickening dusk, the dark red brick of the terrace opposite. Hearing the train crossing the viaduct, heading for the city we'd left behind.

'Garda,' she said. 'Is that one?'

'And Maggiore. Lake Maggiore.'

Something to say, to fill the gap. To conjure up a sunny but far-away place that couldn't easily be put to the test and found wanting. More than that, might just be worth the effort. I repeated it, like a seduction. 'Mm, Lake Maggiore.' To try to convince us both.

We lay there, thinking the same thoughts. Here and now might be a disappointment, given the build-up, the expectations, the fall-out. But perhaps it wasn't our fault, not deep down. We'd surely find our real selves over there, freed from this confinement, the weight of dark brick and guilt. We made mental pictures of ourselves standing together by the blue waters, feeling the warm stones under our feet, looking over to the green slopes, the crags and peaks beyond. As though our better selves had already taken up residence at the villa behind us (dazzling white, colonnaded, the bougainvillea tumbling over its terraces) and would be there, at the entrance, to welcome us, to show us how it was done.

'They do flights from Cardiff,' I said.

'And connections?'

'I'll find out.'

Pause. 'I wouldn't want to chance it.'

'There'll be packages,' I said. 'All in. Flight, transfer, hotel. The lot.'

'It would spoil it. If I had to worry about ...'

We lay there and made our pictures again. I turned to Clare and put my hand on her hip, pretended that the 'all in' had already begun, that the decision was as good as the act. I kissed her. Stroked her belly. Then kissed her belly, too, its skin soft and silky on my lips. Smelt our sex.

'You'll get the brochures?' she said.

'Tomorrow. Lunch-time. I'll call in at Thomas Cook's.'

Then quiet again. We lay back and felt the dusk gather around us.

'Not too early, though.'

'Eh?'

'The flight. I wouldn't want a flight too early in the morning.'

'No, of course.' I thought about this. 'What's too early?'

'You know. They say ten. But you've got to be there two hours before. And then there's the drive over. So you've got to be up at five. That sort of thing.'

I felt like saying, 'It was your idea, not mine.' But I just nodded. By then I didn't know whose idea it had been. I knew only that the gap had been filled, we had found a serviceable decoy for the thing that was missing.

I am still reading my complimentary copy of *The Times*, glancing occasionally through the window to pick out the features which the pilot identifies. The English Channel. Paris. And now, the foothills of the Alps.

I have brought a copy of Lampedusa's *The Leopard* with me in my hand luggage, thinking I might start it during the journey, to get me into the mood. Instead, I read the Sammy Davis Jr obituary, then browse vacantly through the sports section, follow the build-up to the World Cup semi-final, which I have reconciled myself to missing. I wonder whether I might catch it after all, if I play my cards right. Then, unaccountably, I turn to the business section. For a few minutes I ponder the rise in inflation, the changes in insurance regulations, the economic impact of BSE. And I think to myself, what the hell? What else is a holiday but this? To lose oneself in the business section of *The Times*, content in the knowledge that it is all of no matter. Nothing matters because all obligation has been deferred.

Clare sleeps.

I collected the Thomas Cook brochures from town. In addition, feeling that such an important vacation ought not to be chosen on a whim, I got information through the post from more specialist operators like Collett's and

Waymark. This was also, to my way of thinking, part of the fun. Clare seemed happy to indulge my boyish enthusiasm. For the next fortnight we spent whole evenings considering the options, drawing up shortlists, trying to inhabit the increasingly indistinguishable photographs of lakes, mountains and villas.

Clare rejected the specialist operators early on as being too prescriptive and too strenuous. For my part, I gave the thumbs down to Salo and Riva and the other major resorts. If we didn't want strenuous then surely we didn't want busy either. We neither agreed nor disagreed, but we understood there were boundaries and moved on more cautiously.

'Orta?'

'Or Stresa, for the cable car.'

'Mm ... and the Alpine Gardens.'

'Let me see.'

'Look. The islands.'

' "... the three beautiful Borromean islands of Bella, Madre and dei Piscatori ..." '

Perhaps anxious that Stresa, although far away and beautiful, might still not be far enough away, we imagined ourselves sailing to Isola Madre, disembarking, walking its shores, making it our own.

'How big, would you say?'

'Don't know. Barry Island?'

'No, smaller. More like Sully.'

'But you can walk ... I mean, right round?'

I shrugged. We paused to consider what we would do next, after we'd circumambulated our final retreat.

'It looks quite built up.'

'Gives us a choice, though.'

In this way we mapped out our possible days: a mountain, a cathedral, an island, a longer boat trip, then perhaps the marble quarries at Baveno. And in between our excursions, a glimpse of the two of us at a small round table, a bottle of wine already half empty, the waters lapping nearby. And the words, too, beginning to flow as we found something, at last, to talk about, without having to think, What next? What now?

The planning filled a gap. It didn't take the place of sex but it made it less important. Our gaze now firmly fixed on some other place far beyond our drab room and its brick horizon, the sex probably got better, or at least our preoccupation with its deficiencies receded. We were talking, breaking the bread of our words, anticipating that round table by the lake. No matter that the words were scripted by others, feeding our fantasies for their own gain. In the absence of something better, something more truly our own, it was a kind of affirmation.

In the end, we discarded the islands and the cathedrals and settled for Bardolino. It was cheaper. The hotel—small, uncolonnaded—seemed pleasantly situated on the hillside above the lake, away from the hustle and bustle. And there was availability in May. This suited our work arrangements. It also promised more tolerable temperatures. It seemed meant to be.

Mont Blanc draws into view: a flattened, pocket-sized version of itself, over which one could confidently step then stride off to the Mediterranean for a quick dip. But white and cold. And if cold down there, how much colder up here, despite the sun. Bone-breaking cold, just beyond that thin, bolted outer skin.

I see water. The sky is a great blue dome, empty and pure, but there are drops of water on the wing all the same. Little rivulets. Perhaps even the bluest sky is awash. No, not quite rivulets. The drops on the wing are more like strings of beads. Ice? It's hard to tell. But that would make sense, up here, in the cold. And then, a few inches to one side, on the lip of the engine casing, I notice something darker: an oval patch, about the size of an egg. At first I think it is merely discolouration of the metal: rust, perhaps; or else the site of some minor repair. I cast a glance through the window opposite, hoping to find its partner, confirmation that this is in fact how things are meant to be, but I can see only the tip of the starboard wing. When I look through my own window again, the dark patch has changed shape. The egg has elongated and spread.

I consider asking Clare's opinion, but she is still asleep, or at least her eyes are shut. And in any case, what would be gained? I wonder whether anyone else has noticed. I think the man in the aisle seat is probably at the wrong angle. He would have to lean over Clare before he saw anything. I tilt my head. The woman in front is immersed in her guidebook; her partner chuckles quietly at the in-flight entertainment. I consider looking behind but I'm unsure whether I can successfully finesse such an intrusive gesture. They are a young couple, judging by their voices. They have a small child with them who is beginning to whine. Perhaps I could turn and ask, in a matter-of-fact sort of way, 'What time are we due to land again? Sorry, I've mislaid ...' And then venture a little supplementary, 'I don't suppose you've noticed ... It's probably nothing ...' The presence of the child deters me from this course of action.

The aeroplane changes course, just fractionally. The sun now catches the inside edge of the engine casing. The oval patch acquires a coppery sheen. It is no longer a patch but a viscous bulb. Am I looking at petrol or oil? I rummage in the pocket on the back of the seat. The safety instructions make no mention of engines or oil. The in-flight magazine carries a profile of the new Boeing 737-500, which may or may not be the aircraft I am now occupying. It boasts the model's fuel efficiency, its worldwide popularity, from Russia to Argentina. This is not the place to mention oil leaks. And an engine is just a means to an end.

An attendant passes by with a tray of refreshments. I shall tell her. I shall catch her eye on her way back to the galley and say, 'Excuse me. Can you see ...? It's just a little dark patch ...' She will have to lean over then and I'm not sure whether that will be possible. Clare will have to get up. The man in the aisle seat, too. And with what effect upon the other passengers? 'What was that, sir? On the engine, did you say?' I shall have to avoid saying 'engine'. 'Oil', too. I shall perhaps just make a discrete 'come here' gesture with my index figure, then point. The others might think I'm merely enquiring about some topographical feature. And then, when she's leaning over, I shall whisper in her ear, calmly. 'Can you see the little dark patch?' And wait. They will divert us to another airport. Geneva, perhaps. Or Milan.

The attendant walks back. I say nothing. Fearing I might, despite myself, catch her eye, I tidy the in-flight literature in its pouch, I check the time, I look through the window again. The bulb has thickened and spread. It is beginning to break into little eddies. Can I see spray? A faint mist? Yes, they will divert us to Milan, more than likely. But wherever, there will be procedures to follow. Emergency measures. Safety precautions. Perhaps there'll even be a minor incident. The viscous coppery bulb, now eddying and spraying around the engine casing, will catch fire on descent. We will have to make an emergency exit. Down the chute, ambulances waiting, just in case. Touch and go for a while. But then the all clear. Deep intakes of breath. Smiles of relief. Tears, even. Then they'll commission special buses and we'll be on our way, grateful for our second chance and not too disappointed that something of a cloud now hangs over our holiday, dulls the lakes' brilliance. Perhaps, beneath it all, content simply to mark time until we return and reclaim the ghosts we left behind. We shall brace ourselves for the flight back, reminding each other that lightning doesn't strike twice ... And that will be its own escape. Back to a lesser folly, without islands or cathedrals or tables with glasses of wine, standing expectantly, futilely, at the waterside.

Clare opens her eyes.

'Are we almost there yet?' As though I'm her dad, it's the summer holidays, we're driving to Butlin's. It can't be far, I say. There are mountains beneath, without snow. A glimpse of sea in the distance.

Or the engine might, of course, burst into flames right here, in mid-air. That must be possible, too. A spark, even just the heat by itself, and the little slick will carry the flame back to the engine, and from the engine to the fuel tank. There will surely be a mechanised response. The engine will cut out. Sensors will tell the valves to shut. The tank will be smothered in foam. Something of that sort, anyway, because it must have happened before, and they will have learned their lesson. Nothing in the in-flight magazine, of course, but it will be there, no doubt about it, in the specification, in the user's manual. Then we shall limp along on one engine, tilt a little on descent, scrape the tip of a wing against the asphalt. A good story. We could live on that for a week.

She leans over me and has a look for herself. Will she see? And if she sees, will she say?

A Lost Leader

I first met Terry in 1984. It was a bright summer afternoon, about five months into the miners' strike. We both got onto the train at Llanelli. I was travelling back to Cardiff after a day's cycling around the south Carmarthenshire coast. He, it transpired, was bound for Neath. We had not spoken at that point, but I'd noticed his bright orange jacket. I thought, at first, that he might not be a passenger at all, but engaged on some railway business. Track maintenance, probably: something requiring high visibility.

I sat at the back of the carriage, near the door, holding on to my bike with one hand, the *Western Mail* in the other. I read about the death of Richard Burton. The train was already quite full. Most of those travelling were families returning from their holidays. I detected a few Irish accents. They must have come over on the ferry and joined the train at Fishguard. A few minutes into our journey, the guard came to check my ticket. He tossed me some quip about punctures, which I only half caught, then made his way down the carriage. In a short while he came to Terry. When the two of them struck up a conversation I concluded that my earlier suspicion had been correct: they were indeed fellow workers. Terry, still in his work clothes, had just finished his shift, was now homeward bound. I looked at him more closely. He was about my age—early thirties at the most—fair-haired, fresh-complexioned, sturdy: ruddy out-of-doors type. Yes, I thought, colleagues. Checking a ticket was the work of a few seconds; these two were still deep in conversation. The demeanour of both suddenly became more earnest, more animated. I wondered what vexatious railway matters they were discussing. Then, as I returned to my newspaper, I heard the guard's voice, much louder now, but steady and measured. 'It's the right ticket, sir,' he said. 'Right ticket, wrong train.'

'Wrong train?' Terry, too, had switched up the volume. He made it sound like the punch-line to a joke. Gave a little chuckle.

'You've boarded the wrong train, sir. This is the express. Doesn't stop at Neath.'

Terry looked at his ticket, then out through the window, at the countryside speeding by. 'But you can stop it, though, can't you?' Another chuckle. 'I mean, you can tell the driver?' He nodded towards the front of the train. 'Only takes a minute. Up and away in a minute.' Cajoling rather than cross.

The guard repeated his explanation. Terry stared at him. The other passengers looked at the one, then the other, perhaps wondering, like myself, whether the official could indeed exercise discretion in this way. But all he said was, 'You can change at Cardiff.' Dead-pan.

'Cardiff? What's wrong with Swansea?' But no chuckle this time.

'Don't stop at Swansea.'

'Don't stop at Swansea?' Terry stared again, open-mouthed. 'You stop at Llanelli but you don't stop at Swansea?'

'Cardiff it is,' the guard said, and moved on. Some of the passengers gave him a chilly gaze as he inspected their tickets, disappointed that he hadn't furnished them with a happy ending. Others seemed relieved that normal service had been resumed.

Ten minutes later Terry stood by the door where I was sitting. He raised his arms, shook his head, gasped in incredulity. 'But we're going through ... We're going through ... See?'

I saw, through the window, the first Neath sign, then the second. A blink later and we'd left the station behind. The train sped on. Terry looked down at me, incredulous, exasperated.

'We went through ... We actually went through ...'

I nodded in sympathy; shrugged my regret at not being able to intervene. That was enough. Terry sat down opposite me and told me he'd miss his meeting. A whole afternoon wasted, he said. I suggested he might be lucky and there'd be a train waiting for him in Cardiff. Maybe they would delay the start of the meeting. Perhaps if he rang ...? He shook his head and told me his story.

Terry was travelling on union business, which meant strike business. He was a face worker, and lived in the Neath valley. 'Anthracite,' he said. 'Hard coal. Stone coal.' The pit where he worked was a slant-mine, which meant that it didn't need a shaft. Did I understand? No, I didn't, although I might well have guessed. So he explained, with graphic gestures, tilting his arms and hands this way and that to show the lie of the land, the deep strata. Anthracite was the best, he said. The oldest, too, which was really the same thing. Had had the longest time to compress, the most pressure, the most heat. From the time when Wales was where the Sahara desert is now, he said. That was his job. Hacking lumps of coal out of the Sahara. He smiled, raised his eyebrows, invited my scepticism. But what did I know? There were problems, he added, more subdued. Faults and so on. He spent some time describing these and other details I don't recollect.

Then he saw the headline in the *Mail*. We shared our shock at Richard Burton's sudden passing. Terry claimed a distant familial connection. 'Through the Pontrhydyfen Jenkinses.' We reminisced about the early films. I touched upon the recent earthquake in north Wales. 'A sign, d'you think?' he said. He told me about redstarts and ravens and buzzards and golden plovers. As he spoke, I imagined him underground, in his slant-mine, hot as the Sahara. Then I thought of him today, and on all the other days of this already long strike, like a bird, escaped from its cage, bewildered by the light, flapping, threshing, swooping in all directions.

When we arrived at Cardiff station and left the train, some of the home-bound holiday-makers wished Terry good luck, patted him on the back, told him not to let the bastards get him down. One kept us standing on the platform reminiscing about his father, who'd been through '26. A few of the children stared, wondering who this celebrity might be, glad of the delay in their return to normality. An Irishman gave him a ten pound note, 'for the cause'. I hadn't realised so many had heard his stories of faults and raptors, had followed his frustrated efforts to reach his destination. Humbled by these gestures, I bought Terry a drink in the station buffet while he waited for the train. He told me about Radyr stone and ballast, said that's what Cardiff was made of. And the ballast came from everywhere. We exchanged telephone numbers, muttered vaguely about meeting up. I suggested our choir might do a benefit for his local support group.

1989

I saw a lot of Terry during the strike. We did house-to-house collections together around the estates of east Cardiff. You could fit in a lot that way, just in a morning, and the poor were always the best givers. We preferred weekdays. It was mainly women then. They liked his valleys accent, seemed surprised he worked down a pit. Perhaps they'd expected something more scarred and battered, hadn't noticed the calluses on his hands. I think some of them took a fancy to his light blue eyes and straw-like hair, his powerful shoulders. Everybody had a tin of beans for him or a packet of biscuits or a jar of pickles. One old woman gave him her late husband's shoes. 'They were his best,' she said, and turned them over to show there was still plenty of tread on the soles and heels. Then, anxiously, 'Will they fit, do you think?' Terry inspected them. 'My size!' he exclaimed, triumphantly. 'Meant to be!' She was pleased with that. They went into the bag with the beans and the pickles, of course. But no harm done.

And it was a good training, the door-to-door stuff, when the time came. After the strike ended and the pit closed and the redundancy pot got smaller and smaller, he took a courier job for a parcel delivery company. Maybe it wasn't necessary—Kate, his wife, was on a good enough wage at the council, administering schools supplies—but he wanted a reason to get up in the morning. 'And the kids,' he said. One was in college, the other would soon be on her way, and the bills would mount up. But more than that, he didn't want his children to see him idle.

Four years went by and then, out of the blue, he rang. I felt awkward, after such a long gap, but there was no need. It was enough that he could tell me these things and that I was there to listen. We arranged to go for a walk in the Beacons. When would suit? He was flexible. That was the beauty of the job, he said: he was his own boss. Maybe only twenty pence a package, which was shit, but no clocking on and off. No union either, but he was working on that. 'They call me Arthur down the depot,' he said. He'd bide his time a bit, keep his head down, see what was possible.

We met up at Ystradfellte and took the path over to Blaen Nedd. Terry had put on weight. His face was no longer cherubic, just round and now slightly jowelly. As we climbed the Fan Gyhirych track he had to stop every hundred yards or so to get his breath back. He'd put his hands on his hips, look down at what we'd done, take deep breaths and cough chestily into his fist. But it didn't stop him talking. Terry talked all day. He talked about his delivery work. He talked about the perks, how some of the drivers received offers they couldn't refuse and he didn't just mean a cup of tea. 'Like they're just waiting for that knock on the door,' he said. 'As though that's why they'd ordered that bag in the first place.' He talked about underground, too, how he'd moved to another pit after the strike. Ten miles away, and spent two hours getting to the face, and the face so hot you'd think the coal was already burning. Then back to the delivery work. 'At least now I can breathe,' he said. And he didn't have to shit on the floor. He talked about the bigger things, too. What had it all been for, the nationalisation, the marching up and down, the banging on about socialism, whatever that was. All as dead as the dodo. So then the birds. Skylarks now, up on Carn yr Onnen. And the rocks. The escarpment, which we could see stretching out in front of us now as we passed through the notch between Fan Gyhirych and Fan Fraith.

He talked, and didn't stop talking, except to light up. Light up, inhale, cough, then, 'But I'll tell you this ...' And off again. The Chartists' Cave, away on the right somewhere, beyond the horizon. William Price and his son, Iesu Grist. So then the old bridge at Pontypridd, not just because of Price but also because he claimed common ancestry with the man who built it. And concrete which, contrary to popular belief, wasn't a sixties invention at all but was used by the Romans. Rome itself had been rebuilt with it, after the great fire. Then, because we were approaching gorse bushes and could hear the buzzing, the life cycle of the honey bee. But after that, stone again. Sandstone, limestone, granite. And quarrying. And building. And hardcore. And ballast. And the connection between coal and ballast and everywhere, and how he and Kate and the kids had blown £5000 of their redundancy on a cruise to Greece, and so hot they rarely surfaced. Stayed below. Just like ballast. Keeping an even keel. Stayed down with the engines, their steady bleat.

I thought he was coping well enough. Upbeat, at least, all things considered. It's true they'd put him on medication —he mentioned this in passing—but it was only a temporary measure, he said, something to keep him steady until, you know ... Until what, exactly? Until he'd adjusted, he said. Fair enough, I thought. I'd read of miners who'd topped themselves after the strike. Or turned to drink. Or lost their families. So this seemed alright. Coming down the south ridge of Fan Llia, seeing the sea down south, hearing the skylarks again, it all seemed as good as you were likely to get.

1992

Terry's highs and lows continued, the gradient between them steepened. I'd only seen the highs, thought that was him coping. It was hard to imagine an equivalent low.

Kate rang to tell me he'd gone into hospital. 'As a voluntary patient,' she said. Which meant he could leave when he wanted. And work? The delivery job had finished three months ago. Terry's car was found up on the mountain above Maerdy. He'd left it unlocked, door open and full of parcels. Terry turned up later in Rhigos, trying to find his way home, in distress by then and night coming on. Nothing was stolen from the car, but the rain got in and damaged the parcels, so he still lost his job. That's when he admitted himself into hospital. He did so, as you'd expect, with something like zeal, rolled up his sleeves for the next campaign: a different enemy this time, but the same determination to resist. They were monitoring him now, Kate said. Checking his medication, even considering surgery. But that was the last resort, if all else failed. I asked her, 'Can I visit?'

The hospital was being run down, even back then. It was all long, empty corridors, peeling paint and the echo of receding footsteps. So I was surprised to see Terry's ward so full. We sat in an alcove and talked: about the recent election, Kinnock's resignation, the gloomy prospects for Tower colliery, the fact that we were still paying compensation to the old coal-owners for the 1947 nationalisation. And then our last outing in the Beacons, which he remembered well. He fancied a trip out to Clydach Gorge next, to see the old ironworks. He lent over. There was somebody in from Brynmawr, he whispered, and nodded discretely towards the other side of the room.

'With the long hair?'

'That's him. Don't look. Says he sang with the Yardbirds.'

'It's possible,' I said.

Terry shook his head. 'Thinks they've put him in the wrong place. He'll be wanting you to take him home with you.'

A few minutes later an assistant wheeled in the dinner trolley. I got up to leave but a nurse said no need, it was quiet, so I could stay if I wanted. Terry sat down by his bedside table. I sat on the bed. The assistant brought a tray. Terry passed me his orange juice: didn't like sweet before savoury, he said. He considered the other two dishes: one a plate of fish with boiled potatoes and peas, the other a bowl of what I think were prunes but it was difficult to tell because they were smothered in custard. I was surprised to see that the three patients opposite were observing him closely and now followed suit. They, too, pushed their orange juices to one side. Then, unaccountably, and before I could intervene, Terry took hold of the bowl and spooned its contents, both prunes and custard, onto his fish supper. The three others did likewise. Only after Terry had tasted a mouthful, winced and put his tray to one side, did they display any uncertainty. They looked at each other, knife and fork in hand, wondering perhaps whether they too should take a bite, if only to wince on their own behalf and push their trays away from them in the approved manner.

At the other end of the ward the man with the long hair who claimed to have sung with the Yardbirds saw none of this. 'Fine fish,' he declared. 'Friday's dish is a plate of fish!' Terry lent over. 'See what I mean? See what I've got to put up with?' And then, 'I won't be staying here long. Not amongst this lot.' He wanted to get back to his garden. It wasn't fair on Kate. And the back wall needed looking at. Helen, too. She'd be graduating soon. So that was another thing. The wall. Helen. Getting the kidney beans in. The wall. And a trip up to Clydach Gorge. Have to pick a good day, though. Wait for better weather. 'Don't know fuck all here,' he said. 'Waste of fucking time.' Up to Clydach Gorge, get out on the hills, see the old ironworks.

He smiled at the assistant. Apologised for leaving his fish. Asked if he'd have to eat it for breakfast. She shook her head and tutted. Terry laughed. The three patients opposite laughed. 'And me?' one said. 'What about me? Fish for breakfast for me as well, is it?'

1996

Terry died at the age of forty-four. He'd had fifteen years underground; nine weren't enough to dig himself out again. We were still compensating the coal-owners, or by now the descendants of the coal-owners, their surrogates and their parasites, even though there were no pits left. Anyway, Terry had nothing to give them. They'd used him all up.

Learning Scriabin

Do you have a piano to hand? Or a harp? An accordion will do. In fact, you can use any instrument you like, so long as it will allow you to play the following chord. But the piano is best, because this is the instrument for which the chord was written. Here it is.

Go and play it now, if you can. This chord—not some close approximation, mind you, nor an inversion, but this precise chord—is the indispensable backdrop to the story that follows. It is straightforward to play: the notes sit easily under each hand, the intervals between them quite regular and undemanding. Play it, and then, with your mind's ear, try to hold on to its very particular sonorities. This may prove more difficult. Yes, the chord looks innocuous enough, perched on its neat staves. Nor are the fingers daunted. The ears, however, are a different matter. To the ears, it is a slippery customer indeed, hard to capture, pulling first this way then that, refusing to sit still and behave itself like a chord ought to. So do not be surprised if one of the inner notes slips its moorings, if you start thinking, is that really B♭ I'm hearing now? Because it's so tightly wrapped in those folds of harmony. Don't be surprised if you wonder, do I actually hear the C and the D together, or is it just one, then the other? Despite your best efforts, does the mind try to simplify, to bowdlerise? You mustn't lose heart. I was the same myself, at the beginning. Just go back and try again. Play it over and over, until it fixes itself. But perhaps I underestimate you: you may well have an advantage over me in this regard. I am a mere amateur where music is concerned. If you do capture it, hold it tight: it contains hidden treasures.

Years ago, when I was living in Aberystwyth, when the children were small and the sea was blue, I would go and visit my friend Huw Weston. I call him my friend for the sake of convenience only as I'm not sure how best to describe such a relationship. And perhaps that is as good a word as any. No, not friend. Convenience. For this captures well enough the essence of our connection. A creative convenience. Our weekly meetings had one purpose and one purpose only: to afford us the opportunity to play duets on the piano. Every Friday evening at half past seven I would walk over to Pen-bryn, Cliff Terrace and there, for exactly two hours, Huw and I would share, not so much each other's company, but rather the eighty-eight keys of his splendid 1935 Bössendorfer.

Pen-bryn was, without exception, the venue for these sessions. Although there was an upright piano in our flat on the prom that served my own purposes well enough, it could not compete with the glorious resonances of Huw's instrument. In addition, one of our neighbours was prone to headaches. She could barely tolerate the tentative *sotto voce* of my own two hands: four would have been torture. And to be brutally honest, I was not keen on bringing Huw into the orbit of our settled domestic routine. It was easier going to Pen-bryn. There I could retain a measure of control. Once I'd had my fill of duets—and of Huw—I could beat a safe retreat.

Music-making, therefore, was the sole and sufficient basis of our intercourse. We had no other interests in common and our conversations were, as a result, sparse and functional. So, if you asked me, Well, what kind of person was he, this Huw Weston, I should find it difficult to give you a rounded answer. Physically, he was unprepossessing. His slight build, his thin nose, his fussy little movements gave him a rather mouse-like appearance: an appearance aggravated by the monotony of his dress. His preference was nearly always for grey shirts, grey trousers, even grey socks. When his hair eventually turns grey, the disguise will be complete.

What else can I say about Huw? Well, he worked as an assistant in his father's pharmacy in town. I should point out, however, that he was rarely to be found in the shop itself but confined himself largely to the back room, where the prescriptions were prepared. I would often call in, to fetch some medicine or other for the children, and see him through the hole in the wall, marshalling his packets and bottles with busy fingers. And it was no bad thing, perhaps, that Huw rarely ventured beyond this secure little cloister, for what could he possibly have to say to the old pensioner who wanted a little gossip with his tablets? How could he possibly share the joys of the new mother, the grief of the recently bereaved? Huw was simply not equipped to deal with such matters.

And that, I suppose, is something else I can say about him. Indeed, I can confidently declare, without the least hyperbole, that Huw was the most taciturn and least sociable creature I have ever encountered. I cannot judge, one way or the other, whether he was particularly bashful amongst women for the simple reason that, with the sole exception of his mother, I never saw him in female company. But there again, I think he rarely shared human company of any kind. In the back of the chemist's shop or in his parents' parlour: that's where Huw spent most of his time. He was a little grey mouse, with two little grey mouse holes.

Huw still lived at home. The piano had been his mother's, and her mother's before her. 'Your grandmother played at the Wigmore Hall once,' said Mrs Weston. 'With Joseph Szigeti. Didn't she, Huw?' And I had the impression that little had changed at Pen-bryn since that distant but still vividly remembered time. 'Yes. Joseph Szigeti. Do you remember him, Tony?' Between the mahogany candlesticks on the mantelpiece, the dark brown chairs and the painting of an eternally surprised owl, peeping down at us from its leafy perch, it was easy to imagine that Grandma had merely slipped to the bathroom and would be back in a trice, smelling of *eau de Cologne*, to entertain us with a little *bagatelle*.

'From your grandmother you got your nimble fingers, didn't you, Huw?' said his mother, meaning, I think, his musical talent. Huw didn't answer. And because his grandmother had died more than ten years since, I had no opportunity to put this assertion to the test. But whatever the provenance of Huw's abilities, one thing is certain: he did little to cultivate them and, as far as I know, he never tested his prowess in any arena other than his own front parlour. I suspect that this was a general trait. He spurned ambition. He required from life only his own secure little refuge—a place neither too warm nor too cold, too damp nor too dry—and the freedom to reside there without disturbance.

Despite his lack of application, Huw's technique was surprisingly robust; sometimes, in fact, you might say it verged on the virtuosic. He could throw off a Bach *Partita* or Chopin *Ballade* with fluency and aplomb, and made few errors. I must own up to feeling a certain amount of envy at the time—of irritation, even—that Huw should possess such skills, having done so little to acquire them. Although I have practised long and hard for many years, I cannot say that I ever mastered a single piece.

Every Friday evening, therefore, for a period of some two years, we would work our way through Mozart's sonatas, Dvořák's Slavonic Dances, Debussy's *Petite Suite* and other favourites from the classical repertoire for four hands. On occasion, when the wind was in our sails, we'd have a stab at the Schubert *Fantasie*. Holding our breath, we'd do our best to capture the butterfly delicacy of its opening phrases (the Lupu/ Perahia recording hanging tantalisingly in my mind's ear). We'd try to achieve the smooth legato, the subtle colourings, necessary to make of each simple melody something truly captivating. We'd brace ourselves to negotiate the crags and fissures of that final double fugue.

Huw, of course, played the *primo*, in this and in most other pieces. Indeed, he seemed to take the arrangement for granted, as though it were his birthright. I was too polite to protest—it was his piano, after all, in his home—but I did, on occasion, steal a march on him. Whilst he was still busy getting the music together, or fetching the standard lamp, I might commandeer the upper reaches of our double stool. 'You don't mind, do you, Huw?' I'd say. How could he object? And if you judge this to be rather childish behaviour, remember that I was doing no more than respond in kind to his own childish presumptions. Whatever his accomplishments, whatever the merits of his instrument, Huw had something of the self-centredness of a small boy who has not yet had to struggle—and compromise—for his place in the world.

As I said before, these were not social occasions. There was little chit-chat. We would, it is true, have a tea-break after an hour or so, but the conversation never strayed further than the merits of this or that composition, which pieces we might order through the new music shop in town, and similarly mundane matters. In fact, I had longer conversations with his mother than I ever had with Huw himself. Mrs Weston was a stout woman of genial disposition who baked her own Welsh-cakes. (These were very tasty, too, with plenty of butter and spices in them.) For his part, Huw would only retreat further into his shell when his mother entered the room, as though her presence embarrassed him. As I say, just like a peevish little boy.

At the end of my time in Aberystwyth, I said goodbye to Huw and his parents and promised to call by if I happened to be in the area, for a chat, perhaps even for a *tonc* on the piano. But I knew these were empty words. I found myself in Aberystwyth many times during the ensuing years, but I never thought to call in at Pen-bryn. As I have already explained, our relationship was no more than a convenience for us both: a means by which we might achieve something else, something not to be confused with friendship.

After moving to Cardiff, I soon found other duettists with whom to make music, and their company proved a great deal more congenial than Huw's had ever been. All, I'm glad to say, were sufficiently mature and courteous to relinquish the *primo* at reasonable intervals, and to do so voluntarily, without me having to resort to childish pranks. In the light of these new acquaintances, I quickly came to see what a surly, uncouth creature Huw Weston had been. And why should I wish to revive a friendship where, in fact, no friendship had ever existed? I am sure Huw was of a similar mind. I received no word from him in twenty years.

But Huw had, in fact, already re-entered my world without me knowing it.

No-one can live long in Cardiff without realising that it is a city of two halves, divided by a river, and that the residents of one half rarely trespass on the territory of the other. One shops in Cowbridge Road or one shops in Albany road: it would be eccentric indeed to cross town simply to appreciate the slightly different disposition of the same outlets. Why should the starlings of Canton flock to

Roath when they have more than enough roofs of their own to perch on? Perhaps it was only to be expected, therefore, that Huw and I did not bump into each other sooner. Although he had lived in Cyncoed for almost fifteen years, and I had been in Pontcanna for a similar period, each kept largely to his own chosen enclave. Nevertheless, from time to time, one must go to the city centre. It is only from the central library that sheet music can be borrowed. It is to St David's Hall one must repair for the top orchestral concerts. And here, too, in the city's covered market, is the only outlet that sells bags for the Hoover Z1610. I undertake this errand no more than once every six months. But, as I was to find out, this too was Huw's practice. Which served to prove, I suppose, that we had something else in common after all, apart from our love of the piano. And it was by dint of that 'something else', the Hoover Z1610, that Huw and I resumed our old partnership.

I was paying for my bags when Huw saw me. I don't think I would have noticed him otherwise. And if I had noticed, I dare say I might well have tried to evade him. Yes, even after all those years, I suspect indifference would have got the better of me. But fate had ordained otherwise. Huw saw me first. And he greeted me with such warmth that I scarcely recognised him. 'Well, well. Tony *bach*. Fancy, after so many years ...' He shook his head in disbelief and looked me square in the eyes until I felt quite uneasy. 'Huw?' I said, doing my best to affect an equivalent sense of surprise, of pleasure at our reunion. 'Huw Weston?' He had aged, of course, but otherwise was unchanged. He wore a long grey anorak and grey woollen gloves. And I felt a sharp pang of guilt, because what right had I to be extended such an effusive greeting when I had neglected him for so long? His smile put me to shame. It was only natural, then, when he asked me to call round at his house in Angus Street the following Friday evening, that I should accept, and that I should do so in tones of eager anticipation. How could I refuse?

And this is how we resumed the old routine.

'Pen-bryn' was the name of Huw's new home, too, although it would be difficult to imagine a strip of land flatter than that on which Angus Street had been built. In any case, I recognised the house readily without help of name or number because there, in the front room window, stood the old Bössendorfer. The lid had already been raised; the music stood open on the stand. Now I don't know whether all musicians are like me but, on entering someone's house—even a stranger's house—and seeing a piano there, I am compelled to introduce myself to it. Like patting a dog when you approach its territory. A piano does not bite, I know, but this is the best analogy I can think of. It's a matter of propriety. It is also, by now, a matter of instinct. So much more powerful is that instinct when the piano in question is an old friend. And if my feelings for Huw were lukewarm, at best, his Bössendorfer awakened in me an unexpected nostalgia: a bittersweet, inchoate recollection of all the old tunes, all the old times that would never return. It is strange what tricks the memory will play, how it will seduce you into treasuring experiences which were far less significant or agreeable at the time.

When Huw opened the front door, I was surprised to see that he wore on his right arm some kind of sling or splint. He had not been wearing it in the market, I'm quite certain. It was mainly black in colour, extended from his fist to his elbow and displayed an array of straps and buckles. And it is wholly unworthy of me, I know, but my first reaction on seeing this object was an overwhelming sense of dismay, a kind of fatigue of the soul, as I realised what was before me. Because, if Huw were unable to play the piano—and how could a man strapped up in this way possibly play the piano?—what alternative remained for the duration of my visit but to talk? To chew the cud of twenty years. To raise the dust of our indifference, stir it around a little, then watch it settle again.

'Have you broken your arm, Huw?'

I pronounced the words with, I trust, the appropriate inflection of concern. My question was sincere enough: I take no pleasure in seeing my fellow creatures suffer. And yet, as I spoke, I was also busily calculating how much time I would have to spend in Huw's company in order to satisfy the demands of courtesy. Would an hour suffice? Half an hour, perhaps, if I could devise a credible excuse and announce it early in the proceedings.

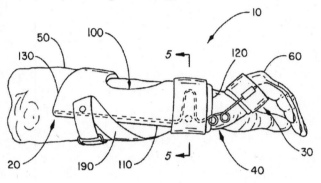

But no, Huw hadn't broken his arm.

'I'd have told you the other day, Tony. In the market. But I was afraid you might not come.'

'Ah.'

'Seeing as how things aren't as they were.'

'Yes, I understand.'

He raised his hand and showed me the limp, lifeless fingers. I nodded sympathetically.

'Carpal Tunnel Syndrome.'

'Carpal ...?'

If this condition is unknown to you, as it was to me, I urge you to refer to one of the many medical websites that describe it in copious detail: its aetiology, its symptoms, its treatment, etc. There is little point in me expounding on such matters here. Suffice it to say, for the purpose of my story, that Huw's right arm had lost all feeling and that he could not even open a door with it, let alone play the piano.

'That's why I've bought these.'

We were now standing in Huw's lounge. This was rather a cramped little room when compared with his mother's spacious parlour in Aberystwyth, and the Bössendorfer filled almost every inch, from door to window. If I felt sorry for Huw, and his affliction, I sympathised quite as much with the piano, poor thing, imprisoned like a tiger in a cage. How had it ever been lured into such cruel captivity? How did it get through the door? Did it roar in protest?

'These are the only things I can play now.'

Huw showed me a number of pieces, all composed, he explained, for the left hand, and the left hand alone. One by Brahms. Two by Scriabin. And a number of others.

'The piano is so important to me, Tony,' he said, emphatically.

'It is, Huw. Of course it is.'

'As Chopin himself said. Do you remember?'

'Remind me, Huw.'

He placed his left hand gently, caressingly, on the lid of the Bössendorfer. '"I now tell my piano those things I once told you." Or words to that effect.'

And although this was only a quotation, and one should not take quotations too seriously nor interpret them out of context, that 'you' hurt me to the quick.

'I'm sorry, Huw,' I said. I meant this as a further expression of sympathy. But was it also, in some vague way, an apology? I don't know.

'That's how it is, Tony *bach*. That's how it is.' And I dare say Huw didn't know either.

Bearing in mind these strained circumstances and my general disinclination to share Huw's company, the evening passed quite pleasantly. Instead of the old duets for four hands, of course, we had to make do with pieces that a pianist would normally play alone. Two of Bach's French Suites. A few Chopin Mazurkas. Even Schumann's exuberant and challenging *Faschingsschwank aus Wien*: a piece I struggled with before but which, naturally, I found much less daunting when I had only the right hand to wrestle with.

Yes, the right hand. Huw's disability restricted him to the bass part, so this is how it had to be. And there was, you might say, a certain poetic justice in this new arrangement: that I could at last, without resistance or rancour, claim the *primo* for myself. The result, with the exception of some slight loss of *ensemble* here and there, and a little confusion when our hands crossed, was quite pleasing. More than that, it was a source of some satisfaction to us both, I believe, that we were still capable of pooling our abilities in this way. And then, of course, there was my own sense of relief. In fact, perhaps it was this, at bottom, that allowed me to regard the evening with such equanimity: my relief that we had, after all, been able to escape to the refuge of the piano.

We broke for tea after an hour or so, exactly as we had done in the old days, when Mrs Weston would wait upon us. And it was quite strange watching Huw do the same, taking on his mother's role. I could almost hear her voice once more, see her round, eager face, as he arranged the cups and poured the tea. I could, you might say, see the shape of her absence. The visible gap.

'And how's your mother, Huw?'

'Passed away, Tony.'

'Ah. I'm sorry.'

'Two years ago.'

'Ah.'

'My father, too.'

'Your father, too? Well, I'm very ...'

'Five years ago.'

'Five years ... Ah.'

If I were a more observant person, no doubt I would have sensed these things earlier. By reading the signs, as it were. In addition to the Bössendorfer, Huw's lounge contained a number of items that I remembered from Aberystwyth: the china cupboard, the mahogany candlesticks on the mantelpiece, the picture of the owl on the wall, and so on. Not all of them, of course, but a representative selection: sufficient to convey something of the aura of their old habitat. They were, I'm afraid, all rather heaped one upon the other, the Pen-bryn in the city being so much smaller than the Pen-bryn by the sea.

We had a second cup of tea and a desultory conversation about our respective circumstances. I did my best to seem inquisitive. Huw answered my questions with his usual succinctness. He was now deputy manager at one of the Boots stores in town. He would take a walk every now and then in Roath Park. His cat was called Matilda. And he would rarely go back to Aberystwyth. 'What is there for me in Aberystwyth?' he asked. And I might have replied, 'Well, what is there for you in Cardiff, for that matter?' But I refrained. In truth, I did not wish to know. It was easier to return to the piano.

Tchaikovsky (*The Seasons*) took up much of the second half of our *soirée*. Then, to maintain the Russian mood, we tackled two of the simpler, slower Rachmaninov *Preludes*, together with a rather anaemic arrangement of the second concerto. Finally, at the very end of the evening, when I was prepared to take my leave, Huw insisted that we steal a quick glance at another Russian: Alexandr Scriabin. Because, he explained, few composers offered such rich rewards for the left hand.

I did not take to Scriabin at first. He demanded an intensity of concentration difficult to muster at the end of such a long and demanding session. Our hands got hopelessly tangled trying to encompass his dense, clotted chords. The outlandish harmonies and sudden shifts of direction made it difficult to map my way through even the shorter pieces. And then there were the eccentric instructions. *Vague. Indécis. Mystérieux.* How was I supposed to play *Indécis*? By striking the wrong note every once in a while? By going out for a quick cigarette between bars? No, it was all too fanciful and *fin-de siècle* for my taste.

Nevertheless, little by little, and much to my surprise, I underwent something of a conversion. In ways I cannot explain, I began to warm to the highly coloured idiom, the unexpected shifts in mood. I began, if not to understand, then at least to be intrigued by those bizarre harmonies. And then, suddenly, one of the *Études*—the twelfth, in D# Minor, the most tempestuous of them all—tripped some inner switch in me, opened some hidden lock, and I was never the same again. How did this happen? Wherein lay the secret? Was it the rising motif of my own part, repeated with increasing urgency, step by chromatic step? Was it the insistent bass triplets of Huw's left hand? Or the breathless, tumultuous, tantalising two-against-three rhythms of the penultimate page? I have no idea. But playing it always left me in speechless wonder.

When we then turned to the two *Poèmes*, I knew that I had been caught, irredeemably, in the Russian's thrall. You would have laughed, I'm sure, had you been present, for the music's glories were cruelly diminished by our halting rendition. But to us, this was of no matter. Playing, after all, is not the same as hearing.

This is how it was for the next six months. I paid frequent visits to Angus Street—not weekly, but regularly—in order to provide a companion for Huw's left hand. Our repertoire expanded to include some of the Prokofiev sonatas (which had been far beyond my competence as a soloist) and even a few tangos by Astor Piazzola (another eye-opener for which I have Huw to thank). We achieved, I think, quite a tolerable understanding, one of the other. Indeed, I believe it would have been quite difficult, at times, to determine, by ear alone, whether we were one or two. If a stranger had strayed into Pen-bryn, for example, and stood in the passage for a while, eavesdropping on us through the door, I wonder what would have been his first words. 'Well, well. Who's that playing? He has a good sense of rhythm, at least.' Or else, 'What on earth are those two doing, playing a solo as though it were a duet? Are they having a laugh?' The first, perhaps. On occasion. That is what I like to believe. That we achieved at least this degree of *ensemble*.

It was in the Mozart that we excelled, and the Haydn, and those of a similar stamp. Nevertheless, by the end of the evening, without fail, we would always return to Scriabin. By now we had both become intoxicated on this composer's heady brew. And if our playing sounded, at times, even more inebriated than the music itself, this troubled us little. The exploration was all: losing one's way occasionally in the treacherous undergrowth was only to be expected. And it was in this mood that we eventually found ourselves tackling the most challenging of all Scriabin's works: the sonatas. It is said that the composer himself was afraid of playing his sixth sonata, describing it as 'nightmarish, murky, unclean'. I believe, in retrospect, it would have been in our best interests to embrace some measure of that fear ourselves.

Perhaps the effort was too much for Huw. Playing with only his left hand, and playing pieces which were, as though to compensate for this limitation, much more demanding than anything he had ever attempted before, he inevitably placed that hand under unprecedented stresses and strains. Try to practice the bass part of one of the Scriabin sonatas for an hour or so and you'll see what I mean. The tendons beneath the thumb start to ache; the wrists stiffen. Is that what happened to Huw? Should we have remained content with our Mozart and Haydn and Schubert and stayed clear of things we could barely understand, let alone play? I'm not sure. Huw isn't sure. His doctor isn't sure. Carpal Tunnel Syndrome is an idiopathic condition, he says, which means that no-one really knows what causes it.

Six months. A time of relative normality, of equilibrium, of simple indulgence in the pleasures of music. And these things, I believe, are not unconnected. It is a peculiar feature of music-making that, notwithstanding the intimacy of feeling it generates, it can do so without requiring us to cultivate any special affection for our fellow musicians. Which perhaps just goes to show that music penetrates to some stratum of our common humanity much deeper than the ego and its capricious likes and dislikes. Yes, six months. Then, after the Christmas break, I returned to Angus Street. I did so, this time, with a degree of pleasant anticipation. Although indifferent at the prospect of seeing Huw again, I was keen to renew our mutual enthusiasm.

When I arrived at Pen-bryn, however, I was once again unprepared for the scene that met me. Why had Huw not picked up the phone to give me some warning? Why did he not send a Christmas card, adding some explanatory note to the seasonal greetings? But perhaps I should not be surprised. The exchange of cards, or of telephone confidences, was not our custom. And there he was, on his front doorstep, ready to greet me once more. Both of his arms were in splints.

'Huw ... What's happened?'

'The other one's gone, Tony. The left arm's gone as well.'

He held his arms in front of him, just as Tommy Cooper used to do, the fingers poking out like little sticks.

'As though they've gone to sleep.'

'But Huw ...'

'Gone to sleep, Tony. I can't wake them up.'

He raised his right arm and struck the back of his left hand with the side of the splint. 'Just can't wake them up.' He raised his left arm and struck the back of his right hand. 'Can't wake the buggers up.' He shook his head, and gave a wry little chuckle, as if his own body had played some dreadful practical joke on him.

We went into the house. I made a pot of tea. Huw thanked me warmly. He could no longer pick things up, he said. Heavy things, like a kettle full of water.

'But how do you cope, Huw?' I asked, thinking of all those cups of tea that Huw would not be able to make during the week, when help was not to hand.

I asked the question in all sincerity, fully expecting Huw to describe how he set about performing his daily routine of washing and dressing, shopping and cooking, getting to work (could he still work?), and the myriad other chores a man must undertake to keep body and soul together. I braced myself for the detailed litany. And I must confess, although it pricks my conscience to think of it now, that, in asking the question, I was already preparing my alibi. That I would love to help out, 'of course I would', but that I was committed to looking after the grandchildren three times a week, that pressure at work had increased tremendously of late, that crossing town by bike was a dangerous undertaking on a dark, wet night like tonight. And so on. Yes, I know it does me no credit, but that is how I felt and the words were all standing in line, ready to trip off my tongue.

But no. Huw said nothing about shopping or washing or cooking. He didn't even mention work.

'Chords, Tony. That's all I can play now. Only chords.'

He extended his arms before him again. I saw what he meant. Huw's fingers, held tight in their splints, arced downwards precisely as though he were sitting at the piano that second, preparing to strike the notes. As though some spell had been cast upon them and they had been petrified, like Lot's wife. And yet, in being immobilised in this way, each hand had, remarkably, assumed the shape of a chord. That is how the splints worked. They kept the wrists, the fingers all in their natural position, their primary posture. As though our hands, from time immemorial, had an instinctive disposition to play chords on a piano.

When Huw said that he could no longer play anything but chords, he was speaking loosely. He meant, in fact, only one chord, and that a very particular chord. On learning more of Huw's condition, I was not surprised at this. If tightening ligaments prevented the wrist's median nerve from communicating with the fingers, from telling them to go this way or that, if the hand itself was tightly packaged in its little splint, this is all that might reasonably be expected. Just the one chord.

'But such a chord, Tony! Such a chord!'

Here I must mention something I didn't fully appreciate at the time—no doubt because of my distress at Huw's condition, my anxiety about his welfare—namely, that he related the dismal news of his deterioration with an unflinching stoicism. More than that, he spoke with an élan, a zest, quite out of keeping with his sad predicament.

'Such a chord, Tony!'

At this point I suggest you return to the piano—or the harp, or the accordion, as I said earlier—and play once more the chord that appears at the beginning of this story. Perhaps by now you will begin to detect in it some inkling of what so excited Huw. As you do so, pay special attention this time to how the notes—the E, the A and the D in the right hand; the C, the F# and the B♭ in the left—lie neatly under the thumb, the index finger and the little finger. For this is the only chord that a hand confined in the way I have described is able to play. You will have to use your imagination fully to grasp this fact, but please believe me: it is true. I witnessed it myself. I saw it with my own eyes.

We played only two pieces that evening: Scriabin's Prelude Op. 59 No. 2 and his deeply melancholic but beautiful *Etrangeté*. Huw chose these compositions because they allowed him to play his favourite chord—his only chord— as a kind of accompaniment. It formed the basis for both: they grew from it naturally, organically, you might say. If they were somewhat awkward to play—our arms had frequently to intertwine in order to capture all of the dense, intricate harmonies—this, somehow, merely added to the delight of our exploration. And that one chord, those tightly strapped splints, lay at the very heart and root of it all.

At the end of the evening, for a while, after working through both pieces many times, the chord was sufficient. Just the one chord. We spent a good half hour playing it together, allowing its elusive harmonics to fill the air around us. We devised different ways of sharing its six notes. Huw played the left hand and I the right; then, swapping chairs, we did the reverse. We went one step further then, sharing the notes in different combinations: Huw, for example, taking the E, the F# and the B♭, and I the A, the C and the D. We achieved a number of other permutations, too, although the choice was, of course, circumscribed by Huw's narrow compass of movement. Strangely enough, although the notes remained the same in the aggregate, the sonorities seemed to acquire new colours, new subtleties, as we rang the changes. 'What is melody,' said Scriabin, 'but harmony unfurled?' And if that is true, what then is harmony but strands of melody woven together? This, I believe, is what we discovered that evening at Pen-bryn, Angus Street, as our ears unfurled Scriabin's most exquisite creation.

'And what then?' asked Huw.

'What then?'

'What can possibly follow such a chord?'

155

I didn't know. Huw didn't know. If I have any ability as a musician, it lies in my sight-reading. Huw's strength was always his technique, his agility, his quick fingers. The mysteries of harmony are obscure to us both. But go back to the piano and try to answer that question for yourself. Perhaps you are better versed in musical theory than Huw and I. Perhaps you have a more refined ear, a keener imagination. Give it a try.

Huw will undergo surgery in the summer to lessen the pressure of the tendons on the nerve in his wrist and thereby alleviate the pain and restore at least some movement to the fingers. I'm sure he'll be relieved to get rid of the splints. The condition should certainly get no worse. Nothing, however, can be done about the damage already suffered. Huw will be able to make his tea again, do the washing up, even cut a slice of bread. He will be able to resume his work as a pharmacist. But he is not expected to recover his musical dexterity. And without the splints, I'm not sure that Scriabin's chord will have the same allure. Will he play it again? I shall never know. I have decided not to go back to Pen-bryn. There is nothing left for us to play. And as I said at the outset, Huw and I were never what you would call friends. Why, then, should I wish to revive a friendship where none existed?

Watching

I returned from Northumberland last night after a week's holiday there with Ruth and two of my granddaughters. I've been home less than twelve hours, yet already my memories of this visit have started to shrink and fragment. In another day or two they will have reduced further. They will still have some kind of shape, but it will no longer be the shape of the experience itself. Everything will have been compressed, transmuted, repackaged into anecdotes for the amusement of friends. Perhaps, in the end, it will all distill into a single image. As though we'd taken just one snapshot. Less than a second's worth. And how can you call that a memory?

I shut my eyes and stand again at the edge of the dunes. I see the sea. The morning sun is already high above the small harbour at Embleton. I see Ruth and the two girls loading the car. A rucksack. A rug. Another bag, with the sandwiches and drinks in it. And off we go. Ruth, Hannah, Lili and myself. Off for a spin in the car. We take the stony driveway from the cottage to the road. Then, when we reach the road, we turn. Which way do we turn? Left or right? Does it matter? Let's say we turn to the left. In which case it must be Thursday. We must be on our way to Lindisfarne, to see the seals. This is their breeding ground; they gather here in their thousands. That's what the leaflet says. Seals. Heads bobbing in the water. Whiskered snouts. Black, impenetrable eyes. I remember the leaflet.

'What do seals eat, Grandpa?'

'Fish, I think.' I've seen them eating birds, too, on television. But I say nothing about this. The birds' frantic flapping.

'What eats seals?'

'Er ... Killer whales? Sharks?'

Lili feigns shock. 'Are there sharks here?'

I shrug. 'We'll have a look, shall we?'

Hannah says, 'Will they have babies with them?'

'It's their breeding ground, so ...'

'Do they kill the babies with clubs here, Grandpa? Do men hit them over the head with clubs?'

It's the girls who are interested in seals. Myself, I'd rather stay amongst the sand dunes. Perhaps I'd catch sight of some of the moths and butterflies that make their home here. The green brindled, for example. Or one of the rarer birds, the summer visitors. Even an osprey. Ruth is more interested in the antiquities. But it's a fine day. We are full of expectation and good humour. There'll be something for everyone. That's what I remember.

On the way we stop at Bamburgh to shop for the evening meal. I like to get this out of the way so we can enjoy the day, free of obligations. I would not relax otherwise. Ruth complies, against her better judgement. 'The salad will wither,' she says. 'The milk will turn.' It's possible. But that's what we do. We buy our provisions and stow them in the boot. 'We'll park in the shade,' I say. 'Just in case.'

After I close the boot I notice an unusual building further down the road. It is built in brick and jars rather with the honey-coloured sandstone of the local vernacular. The Romanesque arch at its entrance, although handsome enough, is much too big for a single-storey structure. I take a closer look. A sign above the arch says that this is a museum, dedicated to the memory of Grace Darling. The name is familiar to me from my childhood. She was the local heroine who, with her father, rescued survivors of a shipwreck, on some stormy night in the distant past. I suggest we pay a visit, in order to 'jog my memory'; although, to be honest, I cannot be certain I ever had a fuller memory of Grace or her exploits. Ruth needs no persuading: she delights in such places. The girls follow, reluctantly. Hannah says that museums are boring. Lili asks for an ice-cream.

At reception, we are welcomed by a bubbly lady in a beige suit. She asks us whether we have come far. From Wales, I say. And then qualify my answer with the puerile boast that I am, in fact, a native of the county, of North Shields to be exact. 'Where in Wales?' she says. 'Cardiff,' Ruth answers, thinking she's trying to draw us into conversation. 'Do you know it?' The woman shakes her head. And in any case, she merely needs the information to compile her visitor profile.

The museum is one large room, crammed with exhibits. All of them—pictures, plates, cups, bottles, jugs, tea caddies, mustard pots, soaps, sweets, candles—celebrate and exalt the valiant heroine. Their antiquity is relative. Grace was already in her grave long before most of these objects were manufactured. In that sense, they are tributes as much to the myth as to the actual person.

'Look, Grandpa, her hair ... They cut her hair.'

Hannah draws my attention to one of the glass cases in which are displayed some ten locks of hair, in a variety of little boxes and lockets, each with its own card, noting the name of the donor, the date of the donation, and so on.

'Yes,' I say. 'But perhaps not every one.'

The locks vary in colour from dark brown to auburn to near-white. Some, of course, will have faded over time. But change colour? Surely not. Hannah raises her eyebrows, opens her mouth wide.

'They're telling lies?'

'Some of them. Only some.'

'Why are they telling lies?'

Why indeed? I've no idea. I shrug. I shake my head.

'Some people like to pretend ... to imagine things.'

We walk on, eager for the reassurance of something more solid, more reliable. Almost immediately we come to the rowing boat, the Darlings' own coble, the very vessel used to perform the rescue. It fills the back half of the room. It is in a remarkable state of preservation, considering its age and the ordeals it has endured. We stand and stare, awe-struck that a man and his daughter could row a boat so large, so heavy, and in seas so rough. And not only that, but pluck from those turbulent seas the hapless survivors and row them back to the mainland. Did some of them lend a hand? To show their gratitude, perhaps? Yes, this is solid. Grace's coble. We can believe in this.

'Is that a real bird, Grandpa?'

But someone, at some stage, must have decided that even the boat wasn't quite real enough, so perched a stuffed seagull on its stern.

'Yes, Lili. It's real. Don't shout or you'll frighten it!'

'It isn't real, is it, Ruth? Grandpa's just being silly, isn't he? You're silly, Grandpa.'

Passing the boat, we come to Mr Darling's diary. We regard it with care and a certain reverence, sure that this is the nearest we can get to the truth of what happened on that awful night. As well as the original diary, the display case also contains a number of individual pages, photocopied and laid out in chronological order. I read two of these, expecting, I suppose, some kind of white knuckle account, a salty, muscular antidote to the knick-knacks and persiflage. But this is not, in fact, a diary, at least not in our sense of the word. It is, rather, the logbook of a conscientious Victorian lighthouse keeper, full of inventories and schedules, a catalogue of foodstuffs, bedding and oil-lamps, their prices and their weights, descriptions of the goods washed ashore from other wrecks, accounts of the money raised from their sale, and so on, all in meticulous and dispassionate detail. I should not have been surprised. This was the job for which Mr Darling was paid: to man his lighthouse, not to reminisce, or service the tourist industry of future generations. There is only one sentence devoted to the rescue, and that coldly factual, without reference to Grace. Ruth notices that Mr Darling makes no mention of his other children either, or even his wife, who died during the period covered by the diary.

We spend twenty minutes in the museum. Then we resume our journey, and do so with some haste. We have only half an hour to reach the causeway before it is covered by the sea. That ought to be sufficient; however, the car in front of us—from Germany, according to the D on the boot—is moving painfully slowly on the windy road. The frustration I felt at the time grips me once more as I write these words: not a memory at all, but a live response, a quickening of the heart. At the trunk road the Germans turn the other way and we reach the causeway with fifteen minutes to spare. Perhaps Ruth is right: I have a tendency to worry unnecessarily.

Then a gap.

I remember the village on Lindisfarne, the cross on the green, the picturesque cottages on either side. The official car park is nearby but we decide not to park there. We have a fair walk ahead of us and there's no telling what mood the girls will be in by the end of the afternoon. So we drive on for a little way and leave the car in a quiet spot just above the harbour. The castle is only half a mile from here: we can see it on its rocky promontory, our eyes click the iconic view. The parking spot also lies in the shade of a high wall. This will keep our provisions out of the sun. Six or seven other cars are parked here, too.

We follow the path. Hannah says she's thirsty. Lili remembers she still hasn't had an ice-cream. At this point we probably take the drink out of the bag. I don't remember. Then a series of stills. A man with a beard and a check shirt and a camera strapped around his neck, clambering over the rocks by the old kiln. A newt sunbathing on a wall. The four of us, still as statues so as not to disturb it. As we start walking again, we see the seal.

Or rather, at first, we see a shapeless black hump half hidden by the seaweed. Then the head lifts, turns. A baby seal. Lili squeals with glee. Hannah hushes her. We all move closer, stepping carefully from rock to rock. The man with the beard is there already, only feet away, taking a close-up. Hannah asks where the mother's gone. Lili wants to know whether the bearded man is going to hurt the baby. As though the camera were a gun.

I don't remember the ascent to the castle. I do, however, have a fuzzy recollection of the rooms within, their high, domed ceilings. Nothing so romantic or extravagant as Castell Coch or Cardiff Castle—in fact, rather suburban when compared with these flights of fancy— but infused with something of the same spirit, variations on a Victorian theme.

A note on the wall outlines the career of its architect, Sir Edward Lutyens. And here comes the bearded photographer again, camera poised. I am peeved at this: that the man should have come all this way, not to enjoy the moment, but rather to reduce it for future reflection elsewhere. That will be the real moment, the one that counts: the inspection of the photograph. It will not even have a memory to jog.

We descend the steep steps. Some boisterous children briefly bar our way. They disperse. Then we see an elderly couple, a little to the left of the path, enjoying the shade cast by the castle's outer fortifications. The man is standing, hands on hips. In his white shirt and flannels, he looks ready for a game of bowls. The woman sits, holds down her blue dress at the ankles. There is a breeze here, at this exposed corner. The man wipes his brow with a handkerchief. As we walk past, I see how fat he is, how much older than I had first thought. A Panama hat lies on the grass behind him. He puffs his red cheeks, dabs his brow again.

We approach three old fishing boats, all upturned, all with doors neatly affixed to their sterns. They are, I presume, used for storage but what lies inside I cannot say. Lili tries to open one of the doors. Hannah scolds her and says she'll be arrested and put in prison. Then she, too, has a go. She tries the others as well. But they are all locked. Losing interest, the girls look over to the rocks.

'Did the mother come back?' Hannah asks.

'And what about the father?' Ruth says. 'Hasn't the father got responsibilities, too?'

I suggest that both the mother and the father must have collected their baby while we were in the castle. And here, on a little patch of grass, we spread our rug, have our picnic and rest for a while in the warm afternoon sunshine. I read the paper. Ruth collects shells and stones. Then I take the girls for a stroll along the shore to look for crabs and limpets. I see no butterflies. I think it's too late for the green brindled in these parts, despite the warmth.

I have ten minutes' worth of such memories. Perhaps less. A memory is such a fleeting thing. A father chastises his son for dropping a sweet wrapper. Two seagulls bicker at the water's edge. We look over at the smaller islands and try, with the help of a map, to work out where exactly the Forfarshire ran aground, and where Grace and her father picked up the survivors. There are many more gaps than memories. Is it on the way back to the village that the fighter plane rips through the sky? Is it by the old upturned boats that I pick up a stone and throw it into the sea? I can feel its smooth coldness as though it were still in my hand, wanting me to throw it again, through this window, to the rain-washed street outside. But that feeling, still so definite, is detached from its moorings.

Before returning to the car, Ruth and Hannah pop into the winery to look for presents. Their purchases—bottles of mead and boxes of biscuits with pictures of Lindisfarne on them—are still here in the kitchen, waiting to be delivered to friends and family. Only Ruth and Hannah go shopping; Lili is tired. I coax her to walk back to the car by promising her an ice cream.

Lili and I sit in the car. I half expect her to fall asleep. If she does, I might well fall asleep myself. Although we have parked in the shade of a wall, somehow the heat has crept in through the floor, through the little gaps at the door and the boot, and settled, so that by now it is much warmer inside than out. I open the windows. I consider opening the boot, too, to see how the groceries are faring. I decide against it. It would be a futile gesture. Best just sit still, enjoy the view, wait.

Although tired, it seems that Lili isn't in the mood to sleep. Indeed, after a minute or two she seems to get her second wind. She takes her colouring book and felt-tips from the storage compartment in the door and flicks through the pages. She points to a picture she has already started colouring in.

'See?'

'Yes, a cow. A fine cow, too. Nice brown cow.'

While Lili turns the rest of the cow brown, I look through the window. Over on the left, about three hundred yards from us, is the Ship Inn. It has a beer garden, which was full of drinkers when we passed by earlier on. Perhaps they're still there, I can't see from here because of the trees. On the right is the corner of the harbour and, beyond that, the sea. Only two other cars are parked here now.

After a while I hear footsteps on the pathway behind us. Then I hear voices. I look in the mirror and see them approaching. The elderly couple. The Panama. (He is wearing this now.) The white flannels. The blue dress. He carries two shopping bags, both quite full; she, only a cardigan, hung over her arm, and a small plastic bag. She is a little lame. I'm surprised she doesn't use a stick. But perhaps it was today she received her injury: no doubt turned her ankle whilst looking for shells. I suspect that's what's in the plastic bag: shells.

'What colour's a pig, Grandpa?'

'The same colour as you, Lili. Same colour as your skin.'

Lili looks at her hands and reaches for the yellow pen. She looks again, at her hands, at the pens.

'What colour's skin, Grandpa?'

The elderly couple walk past us. They walk past the next car, too. Their car must be the one in the far corner, by the wooden hut. It's small and white. A Peugeot, I think. Yes, that's it. They stop. The man puts his bags down, leans them against each other, delicately, as though they have eggs in them. Then he opens the boot.

'You can have grey pigs as well, you know.'

While Lili considers this, the old man takes a pair of shoes from the boot. He leans against the side of the car and steps out of his sandals.

'Are there green pigs, Grandpa?'

The old man puts on his shoes. The sandals go into the boot, followed by the shopping bags. He props these up against each other, as before. I don't see his wife.

'Are there, Grandpa?'

'Mm?'

'Green pigs. Are there green pigs?'

'I don't think so, Lili. No, not that I've seen. But you can make it green if you like. It's your book. Green's fine.'

The man raises his arm, takes hold of the lid of the boot. Does he pause? Is there a gap? I don't remember a gap. And in any case, had there been a gap, everything would have panned out differently. If, for example, he'd stopped to talk to his wife. Or if he'd turned his head to see where she'd got to. Or if she'd called over to him, asked him to hang on a minute, to keep the boot open because she had something else that needed to go in. Just one word, that would have been enough. A second's pause. Everything else would have been forgotten then. The white flannels.

The blue dress. The Panama hat. The rootling around in the boot of their car. It would all have blown away in the wind.

But no-one speaks. The old man doesn't pause. He reaches up and takes hold of the boot lid. He does so without turning his head, without saying a word or hearing a word. As a result he does not notice that *she* is there now, that she has returned from wherever she has been. The plastic bag is in her hand. Of course it is. She would like to put this in the boot, too, so that the bits and pieces are all neat and tidy. A place for everything and everything in its place. And that's all she needs to do: bend down a little, stretch out her hand and drop her bag of shells into the boot. So simple.

And this is what she does. She bends her head and reaches out her hand. At exactly the same time, her husband pulls down the boot lid. He does so in the way men generally do, with a great deal more force than is necessary; indeed, with more force than you would think possible for such an old man, a man so overweight, so red-cheeked. He pulls it down on her neck, or her head, I can't be certain. Doesn't he see her? Doesn't he hear her? Apparently not. Perhaps he feels nothing, either. Nothing except the tension in his arm, the metal under his hand. Pulls the lid down on her head, her neck. She's on the ground now. He's staring at her, wondering what she's doing down there, how this possibly could have happened. Perhaps he says her name. I can't say, but that is what I'd expect. And he still hasn't a clue.

But this is the strangest thing of all. She's down there, on the ground, motionless, but not crumpled in a heap, like you'd expect her to be. Not lying on her side, or on her back. In fact she doesn't look as though she's fallen at all. She's on her knees. Her head and her arms are still in the boot, and she's kneeling on the tarmac, just as though she's about to say a prayer. Or as though she's just rummaging around, looking for something that's got lost.

'Can we go and get an ice-cream now, Grandpa?'

'As soon as Ruth and Hannah come back, OK?'

I remember thinking, she'll move now, she'll shout out. Her husband is an old man, he isn't strong enough to do her any real harm. Old and fat. Sweating again, too. I can see from here. But the woman doesn't move.

'Look, Lili. Grandpa can draw a horse.' I have borrowed Lili's book and pens. 'Can you finish it off?' I do this because I don't know what else to do. If Ruth were here she'd know the procedure. But, of course, if Ruth were here there wouldn't be a problem. She would go over and offer to help, to call an ambulance, to administer first aid. And I could stay here, to look after Lili, to keep her occupied, to keep her eyes averted, until all this is over. And I can't understand what's keeping her. I look in the mirror. No sign.

Lili has drawn a tail on my horse. 'That's right. Now, can you do his ears?'

But perhaps he only caught her shoulder. That would be painful enough. It might even cause a fracture. Collarbone, perhaps. But not so bad as the head. And perhaps not even a break. Just the blow. The shock. Momentary concussion. She'll come round in a moment, in pain, but no harm done. So that's what I say, in my mind. Wake up, woman. Say something. Shout. Groan. Put your hand on your head, your neck, your shoulder, wherever it hurts.

She doesn't move.

'Do you know that man, Grandpa?'

'What man?'

The old man is no longer looking at his wife. He's looking around him, over towards the pub, towards the castle, towards us. Can he see us, inside our car? He's shielding his eyes from the sun. And perhaps his sight is not so good. He's about fifty yards away, and that's a long

167

way, if you're old, if your eyes are failing. Or perhaps the sun is shining on the windscreen, creating a glare, so he can't see us after all. We see the world, but the world can't see us.

'Over there. Do you know him?'

'No, I don't think so.'

'Why's he waving at us?'

I can't be certain whether it's us he's waving at. I look in the mirror and see no-one else. He may, of course, just be waving at random, in the hope that *someone* will see. This seems unlikely, but then, what options does he have? What else could he do? Then he stops waving. He looks down at his wife. For a second I think she's moving. No, I think she *has* moved. He must be thinking the same thing, which is why he looks at her. Says something, too, more than likely. Her name again, no doubt. Does she answer? I don't know. I have closed the car windows. I can no longer hear anything.

'Grandpa?'

Her head has moved. Her head and her right arm. Her head has slipped out of the boot and now lies against the fender. For the first time I can see her face. The mouth is open, but the lips aren't moving. And if the old man doesn't do something quickly, his wife's head is going to slip again. Slip again and fall on the hard ground. And that would hurt. Really hurt. I want to open the window and shout out, Lift her head up, man! Lift it up before it falls on the ground!'

'Grandpa?'

Yes, I'm certain of it now. He's waving at us. He's seen Lili moving. Lili's been sitting still long enough, and she's only four, so she's starting to get restless, and that's all it takes, just a glimpse of her hand, pointing through the window, her turning head. You can always see a thing that's moving. Stock still is the best disguise. Blend in to the background. Yes, it's us he's waving at, and shouting, too.

168

Despite the distance, the closed windows, I can hear his voice. High pitched. Hoarse.

'So, how's about we do a picture of a bird? You see that seagull over there, on the wall? It's like the bird we saw this afternoon, isn't it? The one on the boat, remember? Do you think you can draw a picture of a seagull?'

Her face, lying against the fender. Mouth open. Blood. Not flowing. Gathering. And not red, either. At least, not from here. More black than red. The effect of the light, perhaps. The shadows. Her face is in shadow; his is still in the sunlight, looking down at her. And the blood like another shadow, at the side of her mouth, on her blue frock.

'Ruth and Hannah will be back soon. We'll all have an ice-cream then.'

Talking with the Dead

We called her 'Miskyn Meg'. Facile, but it stuck. 'Meg' wasn't her real name, of course, but she lived in Miskyn and she worked as a clairvoyant. Still does, as far as I know, but she moved to another part of the Vale and we lost touch. One visit was sufficient, you might say. Or perhaps my interest just waned with time. I believe this is often the case. We dabble in such things—mysticism, the occult, cabbage soup diets—but quickly tire as we realise they promise more than they can deliver. Sometimes perhaps we fear they will deliver more than we are prepared for.

Be that as we may, for a few months Miskyn Meg became the subject of wonderment and heated debate amongst our friends and colleagues. It was S, an acquaintance of Ruth, my partner, who went to see her first. She, in turn, must have known someone who'd seen her before that, and so on, but I can only speak for our own group. I know nothing of Miskyn Meg's history. S told of a remarkable woman she'd met who could talk to the dead. She'd chatted merrily with S's grandfather about the games they'd played together when she was little. She'd described trips S and her parents had made to Chester to see Santa Claus. Then, through the tears, S recounted how Miskyn Meg had made contact with an old boyfriend who'd been killed in a car accident near Carmarthen. She'd mentioned about his fondness for *dolmades* and the novels of Henry Green, and a plethora of other obscure and inconsequential details which it would surely have been impossible to glean from even the most assiduous researches.

'Tell me, Tony, was it just curiosity brought you here?'

'Curiosity, yes. But not just that. I also wanted to ask about someone.'

As well as conversing with the dead, Miskyn Meg could foresee the future. Which is, of course, much the more remarkable achievement of the two. We give it less attention, perhaps, only because we cannot assess its accuracy at the time. Another friend of Ruth's, whom I shall call 'P, was witness to this facility. Meg predicted that P's little daughter would fall on the steep garden steps at home, lose consciousness and have to be rushed to hospital. P said that Meg could see the accident unfold precisely as though it were happening there, in her front room in Miskyn: Nia falling, crying out; then P running over, desperate and panic-stricken. And there was pain in her eyes, P said, as she watched it all unfold. 'She took on my pain ...' But Meg assured her that there was no need to worry. Yes, this would happen, if not this week then next. Nia would fall. She would receive the necessary treatment. Then she would return home, none the worse for her ordeal. And that, said P, was one of Miskyn Meg's guiding principles: she would never be the bearer of bad tidings, except only to warn of what might happen if no action were taken or, in this case, simply to offer reassurance that the bad that will happen is not nearly as bad as might at first appear.

So it transpired. And if, despite this reassurance, the mother still screamed when her daughter fell and hit her head, and shook like a leaf when she saw the blood, shook so much that she could scarcely phone for an ambulance, Miskyn Meg could hardly be blamed. These were the instinctive responses of a mother, whether forewarned or not. And perhaps, also, P did not have complete faith in Meg's ability to predict. That is the nature of prophecy. As I said before, you can't prove its accuracy until it's too late. And fear is generally mightier than faith.

Having taken all the necessary precautions, having examined the wound, studied the x-rays and tested the eyes, and concluded that there was no cause for concern, the little girl was sent home, just as Meg had foretold. All were greatly relieved. Only then, when normal life had resumed, did they reflect on Miskyn Meg's remarkable prediction. How could such a thing be possible? And should they go back, to find out more, to allay their fears about this and that, even to ask about the things they did not yet know and therefore could not fear? Did they dare? These were the questions that occupied P's family and their friends that evening and for many subsequent evenings.

'It's George talking now.'
'My father.'
'No.'
'No? But he was ...'
'Don't talk, Tony. I can't hear the voices when you talk.'

During the next few months, more friends went to Miskyn. Although none recounted anything so shocking or so poignant as P's incident in the garden, all testified to the accuracy of most—not all, but most—of Meg's responses. She could recite their medical histories; she even knew what ailments afflicted their children. She referred to Cheryl's astigmatism. She asked after Ifan, who had broken his finger while playing football on the school yard. She knew about every eccentric uncle and kindly grandma who had long departed this life: she knew how they lived and how they died. All agreed that Miskyn Meg had quite remarkable powers.

'Not your father, your grandfather. He's standing ... I think it's a ship I can see behind him. He's got a big smile on his face.'

Despite these endorsements, I was at first reluctant to share our friends' credulity. I am by disposition a sceptic. I have perhaps also come under the influence of Derren Brown, who has shown so graphically how 'miracles' of this kind can be simulated through the use of hypnosis, cunning mind games, elaborate trickery, and so on. Most of all, he has demonstrated how eager we are to believe the improbable, even to seek out that which confounds reason and the evidence of our senses.

'And your brother ...'
   'But he's still ...'
   'Still alive, I know. David, isn't it? He was quite a sickly little boy, wasn't he? Asthma, I think. Yes, that's right. Asthma. Had difficulty breathing. He needs to keep an eye on that. He'll have trouble with his chest as he grows older. And the smoking, of course. That doesn't help.'

Yes, I am a sceptic by nature. On the other hand, I know as well as anyone that the universe is full of conundrums and that we must be humble and open-minded when we encounter them. We need to remember that the ignorance of even the wisest amongst us runs much deeper than our knowledge. So it was with a rather studied impartiality that Ruth and I went to the modest semi on the modest estate in Miskyn to have our session with Meg. In Ruth's case, the humility was mixed with a certain playfulness: she wanted to share the wonderment of her friends. As for myself, I had a more specific purpose. I wished to enquire about a friend of mine who had taken her own life. What had driven her to such an extreme? And what then? Or rather, did such a 'then' exist? No, of course it didn't, I knew that already. And yet I desired, you might say, the undoing of my disbelief.

'And your mother ...'

At first sight, the house in Miskyn did not lend itself well to mystery and wonderment. In the lounge the cabinets and shelves were all densely populated by miniature porcelain animals: sheep, cows, tortoises, pigs, squirrels and so on. Squirrels prevailed: red, bushy-tailed, each grasping a nut in its cute little paws. On the mantlepiece a cat tried, and failed, to catch its butterfly.

I remember these details well because I had over an hour to study them. Ruth was upstairs with Meg and there was nothing else to do except look through the window, at the driving rain, or read the *Daily Mail*. I remember them, too, because finding such sentimental knick-knacks in a place that was supposed to be set apart—hallowed, you might say—discomposed me. I am sure, if Ruth had not already begun her session, this jarring juxtaposition would have made me turn tail and return home there and then. This is an odd confession to make, I know, given that I was a cradle Catholic and well used to seeing the Saviour Himself and his Holy Mother reduced to cheap plastic trinketry.

'But she's ... '
  'Yes, I know. She's alive, too.'

And then, the *Daily Mail*? In my naivety, my snobbery, I was scandalised that one such as she, a communicator with the dead, should subscribe to such a bastion of intolerance and chauvinism.

When Ruth came downstairs she wore on her face the expression of one who had spent an hour in the company of an old friend, exchanging reminiscences, each goading the other to take just one more piece of chocolate cake. Again the evidence of my eyes jarred with the supposed gravity of the occasion. On the other hand, we must remember that Ruth, unlike most of us, is on good terms not only with her past but also with her future.

Meg's upstairs room ('my hideaway' she called it) was furnished more sparsely than the lounge. Two easy chairs occupied the centre of the floor, with a small round table between them. There were no squirrels in sight. Even then, the room could hardly be described as bare: the walls were covered in red chintz wallpaper, the chairs deeply cushioned. The latter were cheap, of course, their luxury only superficial. When I sat down, the imitation leather squeaked in protest.

'Your father's here now.'
  'You can see him?'
  'Your father was George, too, wasn't he?'
  'But what about my mother?'
  'It's your father I can see now ... Yes, and his voice, I can hear his voice.'

Meg hailed from Swansea way, judging by her accent. As I say, I know nothing of her history. Nor did I get the opportunity to ask. Although quite hospitable, in her own way, she was not given to small talk. Her business was to tell you your hidden truths and she was impatient of distraction. Neath, perhaps, rather than Swansea. Or Port Talbot. I'm not an expert on accents in that part of the world.

'Yes, your father. I can see him clearly now.'

I remembered Derren Brown's cautionary words. Hadn't I already confirmed that my father's name was George? What other information had I divulged inadvertently, perhaps through nodding or shaking my head? Through looking this way and that. Through folding my hands. Through unfolding them again. They say that the eyes and the hands can betray you quite as conclusively as your tongue. More so, perhaps, because you're not on your guard. Tricks of the trade, said Brown. The quacks noted every little twitch and fidget and fed it all back to you as miraculous revelation. So, with these misgivings uppermost in mind, I fully expected

Meg to describe what she claimed to see, to detail my father's features. She'd start with the eyes, tending downwards at the corners to give a permanently hangdog expression. She'd move on to the quite prominent nose, where a touch of the Italian survived. After all, I didn't need to say a thing for her to know all this: she could read it well enough in my own face. A quick glance and she'd have it. Perhaps when I came in through the door, when she smiled and said, 'Hello,' and we shook hands. That would have been enough, more than enough. Broad brush strokes, Derren Brown said: that's all you need to keep the audience happy, lapping it up.

'I can see him now. He's in his waistcoat, his white shirt. The room's full of people. Not sure who the others are ... It's very dark ...'

But she's looking at the floor now, not at me. And not at the floor itself, perhaps, but rather at somewhere out of sight, somewhere inside herself.

'He's bending forwards now, over the table. He has a cue in his hand. Yes, I can see him clearly now. He's stretching his left arm out over the table, concentrating on the ball. There's someone else there, too, another man with a cue, standing to one side, smiling, looking at George. Everyone's looking at George. I can see the gold ring on his finger, the parting in his hair, on the left-hand side. Everyone's watching, waiting for him to strike the ball ... I can see his face now, Tony. You look like him, don't you? In your face, I mean.'

I'm not surprised that Miskyn Meg says I look like my father. True or not, it's what I'd expect her to say. After all, sons take after their fathers. But where did she get the ball and cue? How did she know about the billiards?

'Everyone's quiet, waiting for your father to play. I'd say, by the look on his face, he really enjoyed his snooker.'

'Billiards.'

'Sorry?'

'Dad didn't play snooker. Just billiards. Didn't have any time for snooker.'

'I see. Billiards.'

'How many balls are there?'

'I'm sorry?'

'On the table. How many balls are there on the table? Are there three? Are there more than three?'

'I'm not ... I can't say ... It's too dark ...'

I say 'Sorry', for speaking intemperately, for so clearly putting her to the test. She looks uneasy. Her eyes are still shut, staring inwards, but the lips have tightened. She has moved her hands, too: only her finger- tips touch the table-top now, very lightly, as though she were about to play the piano. I apologise again. 'I'm sorry I ... ' She shakes her head.

'The balls have gone. The other man's gone. There's only your father here now. He's bending forward again, but not like before. He doesn't have a cue in his hand. He doesn't have a waistcoat. He's sitting in an armchair, leaning over. There's a table there, just a small table, to one side.'

She is suddenly quite still. Her little head, her little hands, her little delicate body, all are quite still. I want to ask her about the table. Is it oblong? Does it have ceramic tiles on it? And do those tiles bear a slightly raised pattern, like leaves, but in a sort of burnt red colour? Do they? Do they? But my tongue gags on the banality of it all.

'He's leaning forward, holding on to the arm of the chair, and he's ... he's started to cry. Yes, I can see the tears. He's saying "No, not that, no.'

Her little red lips close around the 'o' and hold it there, silently, in the air. And her lipstick is really much too garish for an occasion such as this. I want to tell her, Thank you, but I didn't come here to discuss my family, to hear inconsequentialities about a grandfather whose name I never knew, to see my father playing billiards, and worse, much worse, to see him crying. I came to ask about someone else, someone about whom I cared.

'He's raising his hand to his forehead. Covering his eyes. He's still crying, I can see the tears on his cheeks. "I was only thinking about you, Anthony ..." He's speaking to you now, Tony. "It was for your own good. But not this ... I don't want ... I can't take any more of this.""'

She looks at me. For the first time Meg raises her eyes, looks for an explanation. Which is only natural. My father has stopped in the middle of a sentence. She wants to know why. But I don't know why. I didn't understand any of this at the time, way, way back, when I saw it all for myself. The tears. The hand over his eyes. I still don't understand. How can I? Fathers don't cry. Not properly. They don't know how to do it properly, they never learned how. Once in a blue moon a father's tears will flow and you've got to be there with your little jug, ready to catch the pearls.

'He's trying to talk to you, Tony.'

And how would I reply? 'Your tears will have to be a good deal more remorseful than that, Dad, if you want me to take any notice.' Yes, I might well be up to saying such a thing, given a second chance, given immunity from any unintended consequences. 'You'll need a whole lot more tears, and better tears at that, if you want forgiveness from me.'

'As though he's ...'

Meg looks down again.

'As though he's ...'

And shakes her head.

'I don't understand.'

Of course she doesn't understand. Miskyn Meg, for all her psychic powers, is a respectable spinster from Swansea way, a little unconventional but quite guileless. You wouldn't give her a second glance if you saw her walking through the Quadrant or the Aberavon Centre. She lives with her porcelain menagerie. That's where she's at home, amongst her cats and dogs and squirrels, doing her harmless little circus tricks for the curious and the sentimental. She hasn't the slightest idea about these tears, cannot guess that they are from another world entirely, another dimension.

'He seems to be in some distress.'

'Distress' is a serviceable word. Her word. It covers a multitude of afflictions without sounding too grievous. I should have preferred 'torment', but perhaps it's rather old-fashioned, even for one such as Meg. Nor would it sit well amongst all that lipstick, on those very proper lips. But 'torment' it should be. A good old Catholic word. 'Torment' is a word from hell, and there's no doubt about it: hell is here, in this room. For the man who prostrates himself, who cries tears for the first time, who says (pitiably, but without conviction), 'It was for your own sake ...', knowing that none will believe him, this is hell. For the man who, in his own clumsy, self-righteous way, earnestly desires forgiveness but realises it's just all too late, this is hell.

And how could Miskyn Meg know that? Not just the hand on the brow, and the table, and the tears, but hell itself, the tears flowing for all eternity. Could she detect that, too, in my face, in my fidgeting hands? Was that, too, just a trick?

When I get home I look at my photograph album. He is there, cue in hand, ready to strike the ball. Could she see this, through my eye's lens, as though she too were looking at the album? Could she turn the pages at will? Then I look in the mirror and wonder whether I can see what Miskyn Meg saw. I appreciate that this is a different matter altogether. A man knows his own face too well to read it properly. It takes a stranger to see the things forgotten, shoved to one side, denied. But I look in the mirror, anyway.

I see my father staring back at me.